This book is

- You con   l
- You do   l way
- You are se..   s
- You understand that making mistakes are an essential part of growing
- You are looking for practical advice - not woolly theories
- You are prepared to do what it takes to achieve your goals
- You say what you think, live your own life and make your own choices

Free Bonus Videos on your Smartphone!

To add another dimension to the book, I have created videos in which I add more information  about the subject covered in each chapter. These are free to view and an added bonus that goes with the book. To view the videos, you will need a QR code reader, which is a free app that you can download on your smartphone. Enjoy!

What People Say About Mark:

"Mark is irreverent, refreshingly honest and open about his mistakes and demons as well as sharing his triumphs, and business savvy. Few business authors reveal the full spectrum of their lives so openly and that makes him instantly likeable and easily relatable. Decades of wisdom condensed into the Time Management section are priceless – these tips alone make the book well worth the read."

Kelly Devlin, HowtoGrowaBusiness.com

"A compelling read with some great lessons that everyone can learn from whether you're an Entrepreneur or not. The Rebel Entrepreneur illustrates just how fragile success can be sometimes and just how easy it is to make the wrong decision when you're put under serious pressure to be a success, whether self-induced or external. But if you make the 'right ones', the life you dream of is yours for the taking."

Justin Noble

"This is a great book; Mark's really inspirational. Once I had started reading it, I couldn't put it down. Mark, it's amazing to get insight into your life and the challenges you have faced over the years.

Marketer or no marketer, there's some really good tips and advice for anyone. Interesting, well written and raw, an insight into real life; highly recommended."

Matthew Houghton

"Mark is a 100% straight shooter, tells it like it is and goes out of his way to put other people first including his business partners and most importantly, his customers.

He has great knowledge of marketing and is someone you can do business with, with total peace of mind.

If you're looking to be successful online and build your business faster, then look no further..."

Simon Hodgkinson, Hodgkinson Publishing

"The strategies Mark teaches are very simple but incredibly effective... with a knack for making money against the odds, Mark shares information in an easy to understand way - anyone can follow!

He really wants to make it easy for anyone to replicate his success and as someone who's been there, done it, lost it and is making it again... he has a refreshingly down to earth approach, unusual online."

Pete Craig

"Read this book! Learn from it! Remember that who you are makes a difference, and what held you back in the past is no excuse for creating the future that you deserve."

Nigel Risner, author of The Impact Code

Work With Mark

Here are a few ways you can work with Mark...

Mastermind Group:
Join Mark's mastermind group of entrepreneurs from around the world. Get direct access to Mark weekly.

Private Consulting:
Bring Mark in to consult to take your online business and income to the next level.

Workshops:
Mark is able to run a workshop for your company. Full and half day options are available.

Training Courses:
Mark runs a variety of training courses on different topics

Speaking:
Get Mark to come and speak at your event.

Business Services:
Mark also offers a variety of online business services.

Visit http://marklyford.com/WorkWithMark
for all the details

Sign up to Mark's FREE newsletter!

Get updates from Mark for free delivered to your inbox weekly.

Sign up at http://www.marklyford.com/NewsLetter

About The Author

Mark Lyford is the rebel entrepreneur with a cause; a self-taught marketer with an eclectic mix of marketing and entrepreneurial experiences. He has 15 years' experience as an online entrepreneur and has been in business for over 22 years. His varied and sometimes controversial career began in earnest in 1997, when he seized an opportunity to enter the adult entertainment industry. At the height of his success, Mark was living with his wife and first son in The Bahamas, enjoying his millionaire status and had over 32,000 websites.

In 2002, having dramatically lost everything during a progressive move to increase business, he moved back to the UK, bankrupt and desperate to regain his status. His marital break-up and even a subsequent prison sentence could not make him lose his resolve. In recent years, he has emerged like the phoenix from the ashes of his former career, rebuilding his Internet business and reinventing himself with hard work, dedication and with some inspired creative product making.

Dedicated to his business goals, he currently works as a publisher, marketer and public speaker with a team of loyal people behind him. His public speaking appearances included the recent Marketing Summit event in Manchester and multiple London events. He also creates and presents his own training workshops throughout the UK.

His book *Rebel Entrepreneur: Porn, Paradise, Pot, Prison* is charting his experiences in life and business.

He is currently planning a sequence of strategic business products including RealResults.co.uk, WordpressStudio.net and GetSuccess.com to name a few.

Mark is divorced, he is about to move to a farm in Ashby-de-la-Zouch in the midlands of England with his dog, Dave, and has two children, James, 13, and Alexander, 9.

http://marklyford.com

Disclaimer

This book is written as if I am talking to you and I think it's important that it should be in my own voice because this is my story. With that in mind, there is some swearing and profanity. It's just the way I am. There are some stories in the book that may offend some people but this is me and this is my life. So I am just warning you before you start. I make no apologies if you are offended in anyway. ;)

Dedication

This book is dedicated to my mum and dad
who without their constant love and support,
I could not have lived the life that I have.

No one else in my life has had the unwavering
belief that I can achieve all that I want
and that everything will be ok.

Love you, Mum and Dad.

*"Stop focusing on
what you do not have,
and shift your consciousness
to an appreciation
for all you are
and all that you do have."*

Dr Wayne W. Dyer

REBEL ENTREPRENEUR

PORN, PARADISE, POT AND PRISON – LIFE, BUSINESS AND LESSONS LEARNED

BY MARK LYFORD

Filament Publishing Ltd
16, Croydon Road,
Waddon, Croydon,
Surrey CR0 4PA
Telephone +44 (0)20 8688 2598
Fax +44 (0)20 7183 7186
www.filamentpublishing.com
info@filamentpublishing.com

ISBN 978-1-908691-79-8

Printed in the UK by Berforts Information Press

Contents

Foreword
By Nigel Risner

Approximately six years ago, I received a phone call from someone who was incarcerated in HMP.

There was a gushing call about how my book *The Impact Code* had helped and even changed his life.

Then I was stumped. He wanted me to coach him as soon as possible and would I mind waiting to get paid.

Slightly cheeky, I thought, but I also heard a passion, a willingness to make a difference in the world and thought, why not.

I also said yes, because 99% of people who ask me for support never come through with their side of the deal.

From that moment, I would get emails, phone calls, all sharing some new crazy idea.

Then I got the call I was half dreading; that he was out and he could now afford to see me.

Was I nervous? Yes.

Was I excited? Hell yes.

And since that day, we have spoken often.

We have met often.

And I have coached him; bullied him to make life changing decisions for himself and his two great boys.

Is he a client?

Is he a student?

Is he an entrepreneur?

Is he a success?

He is all the above, but most of all he's a good mate.

What more could I want?

Read this book.

Learn from it.

Enjoy it and remember, who you are makes a difference and what held you back in the past is no excuse to creating the future that you deserve.

Nigel Risner

The Impact Code
www.nigelrisner.com

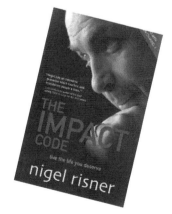

Introduction

Thank you for taking the time to pick up this book. I hope you enjoy it. It has been written with the intention to help people. It's about business and life, lessons learned, what to do and what not to do. It will hopefully help anyone to figure out what they want from life. Entrepreneurs will learn from some of the stories I tell and most importantly learn some big lessons from the things that I did wrong. I hope it enables anyone to think more about their life and what they really want from it. It should provide a few laughs too, mainly at my expense.

Life is pretty short and I hate the thought that 95% of people just exist in this developed world. Way too many people just survive doing what they think they should do without doing what they really want to do, and before you think this is just another 'new age' live your life with passion book, it's not!

My life has been far from normal and you know what, I love it that way! Who wants to be normal? Now that doesn't mean I have no regrets, I have a few. But I know when I look back at my life in later years, I'll be able to smile and think I did it my own way - there is a song in there somewhere.

I have talked on stage many times and some of the feedback I get afterwards is that my message and story is motivational and inspirational. I have read many personal development books but I have tried my best for this not to be one. Life lessons and other peoples' experiences are one of the most valuable things you can learn from. I have learned more from the mistakes I have made than the successes in my life. For me, when I read a book, I am looking to get at least one of two long-term things from it. I hope you do the same.

I have included a few 'Marky Lessons' at the end of some chapters. My aim of these is to get you reflecting on what you have just read and to ask yourself what you can take from this information. The other reason I have written this book is for my own purpose really. It's been a cathartic exercise with many ups and downs as I have re-lived each experience while writing it.

Most of this book was written in two weeks whilst I was in the South of France. I hope it helps you to think about your own life, to teach you a few lessons and to help you to live the life you want.

"In the middle of difficulty
lies opportunity."
Albert Einstein

About Me

"Be yourself; everyone else is already taken."
Oscar Wilde

My family

My friends call me Marky and I was born in Leicestershire in the United Kingdom. My family are normal working-class people who gave me the very best start they could. I was lucky enough to go to private schools throughout my education, something that was a massive sacrifice to my parents as it meant they didn't do other things as a result, such as going on holiday for years.

My parents have always been supportive of me through thick and thin. I have a younger brother and I have two boys, James, 13, and Alexander, 9. I have an ex wife too ;)

I have a large family and without them, I don't know where I would be. Apart from a few brief liaisons, I have been single for nearly seven years now; the right woman just hasn't come along yet.

Oh and I have a dog called Dave. :)

Marky's Thought -
If you have a good supportive family, you can get through anything in life.

The early years

I left school at 16 with one GCSE, (I can only imagine what people thought after all of the private education and the only qualification I got was a B+ in cooking), but private schooling did give me many positive things. It gave me the confidence I have now and it allowed me to see some of the other sides of life.

I can remember when my dad used to pick me up in his Nissan Sunny 120Y car and everyone else was getting picked up in a Mercedes or BMW. At the time I didn't like it, but looking back it was the best thing that could have happened to me. It gave me the best of both worlds. Different and 'real' is good, not like many of the stuck-up kids I went to school with. My third school was the best school I went to. I had much more normal people around me and the parents were 'real' people. As I mentioned, I have a younger brother too; we are like chalk and cheese, completely different people but very much best friends. We have taken very different paths in life. He runs a successful martial arts training business and looks after his two great children. We both grew up as good friends and in adult years have experienced a lot together.

I was the geeky, scrawny kid at school; I didn't get any of the girls and I looked like a nerd. Being at private school meant I was at the back of the class. There were hotshot kids much smarter academically than me, and for many kids being always at the bottom of the class would have affected them in a negative way, but it didn't me. It just gave me my 'fuck you' mentality and motivation that has remained with me since. I didn't like school. I figured if I could simply spell and do basic maths, I was set. I think school gave me the balls to stand up for myself. Many times I used to look out the window and imagine what the real people were doing outside and wishing I was there doing it instead.

I started my first enterprise selling electronic organiser software (that I coded myself) to all my rich mates. Psion organisers were the first 'geek gadget' I ever had. They were cutting edge at the time; all my mates had one and I managed to find a book that gave simple programming for games and software. I stayed up until the early hours many nights coding this stuff (well, I say coding, it was copying character for character of the code written in the book) and making it work :) I used to sell the games for £1 - £2 each. That was my first enterprise.

> ### Marky's Thought -
> ### Never forget where you come from.

My first travel experience

The very first time I travelled overseas on my own was to San Diego, California. I was 18. Through my racing pigeon trading business, I had met a cool guy in San Diego called George Fawcett. George first contacted me in the UK and I became good friends with him. Eventually I hopped on a plane and was on my way to spend two weeks with him in California. Upon arrival, I don't think he realised how young I was; it had never come up in our conversations.

California was great; I loved San Diego in particular. I went around with George to some great places. There was a guy who had been running a $250,000 pigeon race in San Diego every year for many years and I went to see him. I had found my next big idea. I knew of a pigeon race that offered $1 million in prize money in Sun City, South Africa and the whole idea of it excited me.

During my trip to the USA, George had arranged for me to go on a trip to Las Vegas to see some pigeon guys who were doing big things over there. I got on a plane on a Friday afternoon, and boy was I in for an experience I would never forget. First, all the money that was there just hit me. I had never seen anything like it before in my life.

I was met off the plane by a guy who George knew and I was to be the guest of a man who was involved in the casino and hotel business over there. Now there was a slight problem. For some reason George told them I was 25-years-old. I was 18. The guys over there must have thought I was real young for my age.

I went round all of Vegas meeting people and loved it. The guy who ran the casino gave me a bunch of free drinks vouchers to use at the bar. I had never really been interested in alcohol before, but it was free and I had been introduced to whisky by another friend within the pigeon circles called Alan.

So there I am pretending to be 25 (not that difficult, I suppose, because I was way old before my time even back then), and on the last night I have all these free drinks vouchers to use up. You can imagine what happened. I got hammered. I remember an extremely beautiful blonde girl called Jenni who I was chatting up all night. I don't know what happened but all I know is that I was woken up the next morning by the telephone wake-up call and I felt like death. The whisky had taken its toll. My clothes were everywhere over my bedroom, my trousers strewn on top of the TV. I can vaguely remember Jenni at my door but that's it. I don't know if I even did anything with her, probably not as I can't imagine I would have been much use.

So, 10 a.m. and I'm having breakfast with the guys who had invited me. I felt like death! I had to get back on a plane to San Diego that morning and it was the worst plane journey of my life; I felt sick all the way. I clambered off the plane and I will never forget George's knowing smile when he saw me. "So you had a good time, then?" That was all he had to say and indeed, he was right, I had really enjoyed it. That was my first experience of Las Vegas, a city which in future years I grew to both love and loath.

My US trip made me want to take things in my business to the next level. I had seen another side of life and I wanted a piece of it. I have since travelled to many places and I think travel can make you a different person. It's something everyone should experience as much of as they can while they can.

> **Marky's Thought -**
> **Travel as much as you can while you are young.**

> **Marky's Lesson -**
> **Don't be a Johnny Big Bollocks at the whisky bar when trying to impress a cute girl. ;)**

"The world is a book, and those who do not travel read only a page."

Saint Augustine

Life

*"Life is what happens while you are busy
making other plans."*
John Lennon

Life experience

For me, life is about the experiences you have along the way, the experiences you can think back on in years to come, and they make you smile and laugh about them. Or the amazing travel experiences in life that you have. When money was no issue at all for me, it brought me one main thing, many of the best life experiences you could ever wish to have. During my life, I have experienced some things that some people can only dream of.

I think that's the most important thing. Gather as many life experiences as you can and enjoy each one. Some of my most memorable ones are the births of my two boys, their first day when starting school and travelling to the Grand Canyon three times. Then there were the many trips to Vegas, the visits to New York and living in The Bahamas. I have so many fantastic trips, way too many to list.

The thing is this: you are never going to remember that extra few hours you worked or the TV programme you watched, but you will remember so many other things that life brings you.

For me, that's been one of the biggest learning experiences of my life. Realising that money means nothing if you haven't got a life to match it. Some of the best ever life experiences I have had have not cost a penny either.

I have a bucket list. A list of things I want to do or experience before I die. Have you written a bucket list? You should!

Good times

Good times are what we live for. It's far easier to remember the good times than the bad.

Ask yourself this. If you had 24 hours to live, you could think back over your life and probably you would want to think about the great life experiences and all of the good times you have had. You wouldn't want to think about any regrets, would you? That would be the worst feeling ever before you departed this world, wouldn't it? For some people, this is too morbid, but I like to think I'm in touch with my own mortality to think about these things. Part of the reason I always go and see loved ones after they have died is that it reminds me of exactly how short the time is that we have on this earth and that we need to pack as much good stuff into our lives as possible.

Life is short. Way too short. We need to live every day as if it is our last.

"It's never too late to be what you might have been."
George Eliot

Friends

After my family, my friends are the most important people in my life. I don't have many, but the friends I do have are the best. I have never been one to have part-time friends. Having friends, real friends, provide you with another layer of support that you just don't get from associates. I have had many people in my life who I thought were friends. But, in reality, they were either hangers-on or people that just stayed around me during the good times. I have a few other people who I really believed were true friends and yet, have stabbed me in the back. True friends are few and far between, and I am blessed to have the best friends around.

> *Marky's Thought -*
> *Choose your friends wisely, watch out for backstabbing*
> *arseholes and cherish those real true friends.*

My first trip to The Bahamas was when I was 18 and it was to visit my very first mentor, Harry. The island I went to was the Grand Bahama Island; Freeport was the city. Grand Bahama is approximately 90 miles off the coast of Florida, close to Miami, Ft Lauderdale and West Palm Beach.

I will never forget the first time I flew into the islands. I was greeted by Harry at the airport and he took me out for dinner at the local marina. Walking through Port Lucaya, I knew that The Bahamas and its surroundings were for me. There were amazing boats docked and the Budweiser family boat was in town too.

Life in the Bahamas was idyllic. Enthused with seeing Harry, and as work combined with the sun, beautiful beaches and nice people, I knew that this was the place for me and I had some amazing times as a teenager on the islands. One particular trip was during spring break. I was 18 and the island was awash with hot, young American girls on holiday. Amazing. :-)

Life there felt different. I called it the 'Freeport effect'. A place that had changed my mindset the moment I landed. During the early days, I was lucky enough to meet many great people there. One of my particular hare-brained ideas at the time was to do a million dollar pigeon race on the island. I had managed to get Harry to fix up meetings for me and the local hotel was up for hosting the event. One day, Harry made a particular phone call I will never forget.

Sir Freddie Laker

For anyone reading this who doesn't know who Sir Freddie Laker was, just Google him. This man was a maverick of the airline industry and the first person to introduce low cost transatlantic air travel to the masses. He took on British Airways and had the backing of Margaret Thatcher and Sir Richard Branson in the early days. Sir Freddie Laker paved the way for Virgin Atlantic to get going.

One Thursday morning, I was in the office with Harry talking about my new idea when Harry suddenly picks up the phone and makes a call.

"Freddie," he says, "Harry Dann here, how are you? I have a young guy on the island who is a friend of mine that wants to talk to you about a plan he has."

I couldn't believe it! He was on the phone to Sir Freddie Laker! They had become friends as Sir Freddie lived on the Grand Bahamas at the weekends too.

By 1 p.m. that same day, I was on the Laker airline plane from Freeport going to Ft. Lauderdale. I was going to meet up with Sir Freddie Laker himself! "Fuck me, this is good," I thought.

I flew into Ft. Lauderdale knowing that Harry had arranged for someone to pick me up from the airport. Within a minute of coming out of arrivals, a Bentley drove towards me and parked up. I couldn't believe it, it was only bloody Sir Freddie Laker coming to pick me up personally from the airport!

I got into the Bentley and he took me to a hotel where I spent the next morning with him and told him my plans. The basis of the plan was that I wanted to do a million dollar pigeon race where birds fly from one of the southern islands in The Bahamas and then back to Grand Bahama. I spent the morning in Sir Freddie's offices and went through my plan. Sir Freddie was such a nice guy and a big fan of doing anything to help Freeport, Grand Bahama and young entrepreneurs. I asked Sir Freddie if he would fly a jet down to another island with some people on board to watch the big release of birds and then fly the people back into Freeport. He agreed. I had Sir Freddie as my sponsor. You can't buy experiences like that.

The race never happened sadly; there were way too many things in my way, but I thank Harry for even picking up the phone and, more importantly, Sir Freddie for giving a young 18-year-old from Leicestershire the time of day.

Sir Freddie sadly died in 2006. But his legend as a pioneer lives on.

I spent many times every year in the Bahamas with Harry and grew to love the place. Somehow I knew I wanted to live there one day. And in 2000, that day came.

My wife Kate, our son James and I moved to The Bahamas; this was a dream of mine finally realised. We spent some great times there. It was short-lived due to the massive financial losses I suffered later on but at the time, it was great. It took me months to persuade Kate to move out and even longer to persuade her we needed to move back. My association with The Bahamas was not over though.

I still wanted to go back and visit my friend Adam, who is Harry's son, although I am not sure I could live there again for a variety of reasons but I still love the place.

Nothing beats Sunday afternoons sitting on the beach with a few bottles of local Kalik beer and some of the best grilled chicken you have ever tasted. Good times and memories that will last a lifetime.

"Surprisingly, very few people realise the power of having a mentor. Everybody seems to think that they are already the finished article and having a mentor is almost a sign of weakness."

Marky

"I once hired my wife's best friend. Her job was to think of 5,000 porn site names a month. She even had her mother buying her porn magazines for inspiration."

Porn

I didn't plan to get into porn. It kind of just happened. My first mentor, Harry, told me I should get into the only thing making any money online, and to be honest, that was porn. This was 1997. My response to Harry was that I didn't want to do it, it wasn't me and there were too many people in it (I smile as I write this now. I can't believe I thought that back then, it was prime time to make money in the business).

I had set up a property website trying to sell high-end overseas property online. In reality, it was at least eight years too early to be trying such a thing. After about a year of trying with property, I decided I should listen to my mentor. It took me another 12 months of being ripped off left, right and centre in the adult industry to figure out this was Wild West time.

This was a difficult time in my life. I was 22, I had a girlfriend who had a full-time job and I was working 5 p.m. to 3 a.m. driving cabs to pay the bills, I'd sleep, then get up and spend the day on my 'wannabe' porn empire. It was hard going and I had to promise Lisa, my then-girlfriend, that I would do something else if I hadn't figured it out within a few months. Well, a few months turned into three or so. I realised she was getting pissed off with me working hours and hours, and I was neglecting her way too much, so I had the idea of taking her on holiday for a week. I figured we had been together for two years and I loved her so I thought I would propose to her. We promptly went to the island of Crete, I proposed on the beach the very first morning, she said yes and I was happy.

It didn't turn out how I thought it would though; it turned out she wasn't very happy.

About a week before we went on holiday, I discovered a company called AdultCheck.com. They were kind of like an adult equivalent of Clickbank.com where they provided the billing and customer support and took a cut. I owned my sites and used their back-end to collect the money. I put up four sites on their network. There was a process of waiting time for the sites to be authorised. I waited a few days and sure enough, I made over $50 within the first 48 hours of the four sites going live. So I put another four sites together and submitted them before I left to go on holiday. Had I finally found something that would work going forward?

I got back from holiday an engaged man. I checked my stats and bloody hell... I had made over $300 while I was on holiday sitting on my arse on a beach! If I put 10 sites together, could I pay all my bills and stop driving taxi cabs at night? The answer was yes. My first money made online! It was exhilarating.

The only problem was that Lisa decided she couldn't play second fiddle to my online business and within two weeks of my proposing, she had left me. I was gutted for six months. But to be honest, I was dealing with a potential monster business and the money it started bringing in helped my heartache. The irony is that I got my first pay cheque of $452 two days after she left.

Now don't think the porn industry is glamorous. Once you have seen one set of tits and arse, you pretty much have seen them all, and I have to admit the start of my online empire wasn't exactly fully legal. Not that I did anything dodgy, but the first content I used were two CDs full of over 73,000 images. I had to sort through each and every image to get ones that were usable. I spent days looking at porn to get 5,000 images that I thought were good enough to use on my sites. By the way, my first sites looked terrible. I only ever designed 20 or so myself. That was enough, trust me, they looked awful. But they made money. Back then, you could put anything up and it would bring in cash!

I eventually found content producers where I purchased images from them directly, all legal and above board, although there was a grey area in the UK at the time. Images showing penetration were kind of not legal, but those laws changed just in time for me.

I've only ever been to one porn shoot in my life in LA, and one was enough; despite what you may think, they are pretty boring. Seeing two girls making out and pretending to be on a rooftop of a building in an industrial estate wasn't my idea of a playboy or hustler lifestyle.

Fast forward to 1999 and I am rocking and rolling in the porn business. I had scaled this thing up to be as big as I could. I had 32,000 sites! At our height, we were building over 500 'feeder' sites a day. Feeder sites were small sites pushing people to our premium site. Things were good, very good. By this time, I had met the then love of my life, and I was expecting to be a dad for the first time.

Having a company generating over $2,000,000 a year was good, but the guy that was signing off my twice monthly pay cheques was probably making a million a week at the height of everything. Time to take things to the next level, I thought to myself.

I generated all my profits from images (no videos around really then). Whatever I did in the network, I couldn't seem to earn any more. No matter what extra effort I put in, the returns were not coming back. I know the owner didn't like the power I had within the network, and my pay cheques were fluctuating a little too much for my liking. The thing is if we saw a hot new trend for, say, 'girls with braces', we would get all the content we could and fill it within weeks. Some people didn't like this. By this time, I'm living in The Bahamas and living a life you can only imagine being amazing. An office in Florida and the UK, homes in the UK and Bahamas. Life was good.

I had many people around me at the time; some would say it was my entourage. I somehow managed to accumulate a lot of people working for me in Columbus, Ohio; the reason being was that my very first employee was a guy called Josh who was studying at The Ohio State University. He answered an online advert that I put out requesting web designers. He eventually went from being a web guy for me to running my entire marketing for all the companies. Josh advertised for me to get more designers and it went from there; before I knew it I had a dozen people in Columbus, Ohio. I used to travel there once a month and during one of the monthly meetings, I put a plan together. The next level plan. You can read more about this in a chapter further on. Josh and I are still great friends now; he attended my wedding and he is a dear friend that I hold close to my heart.

Some quick facts about me and the porn business:

The best porn site name I ever had was FilthyMidgets.com :) I once hired my wife's best friend. Val's job was to think of 5,000 porn site names a month. She even had her mother buying her porn magazines for inspiration.

I sat next to Ron Jeremy on a limo bus and had a chat with him while going to a party at Liberace's house once. Far too many times, I saw false girl-on-girl action at parties (It got boring after a while if they are only acting).

I used to go to the porn conventions in Las Vegas twice a year. I love Vegas but got bored eventually of the conventions. I also got so bored of going to the porn parties, I started delegating the networking tasks to new guys who were working for me (they loved it).

I have only ever met one genuinely good-looking porn star in my life (see the following pic). The rest of them I wouldn't take a second look at if they walked down my local high street.

Despite the hours and hours of video and hundreds of thousands of images I have seen, I still quite like watching porn ;) lol!

Some people think the porn industry changed me as a person. I am not sure. For me, the best thing I can do is to

look at a fully clothed, naturally beautiful woman. So I don't think it's changed me that much. Despite what you may think, the most attractive parts of a woman are face, eyes, mouth, boobs, waist, bum, legs, in that order. Also I have learned that the quiet ones are normally the most adventurous. ;) (Girlfriends, not porn stars)

Towards the height of the business, my daily work was not looking at naked woman all day; it was being buried in stats and spreadsheets, figuring out what guys (and girls) liked. I had to constantly figure out how we could get more people buying memberships to our sites. At the height of success, I had 14,500 people paying me every month.

Life was good. But it wasn't going to last.

> ### *Marky's Thought -*
> *Once you have seen one set of tits and arse, you have pretty much seen it all. ;)*

The big hit

It's October 2000. I have assembled my team in Columbus, Ohio and we have a meeting that lasts all weekend. The purpose of the meeting is to discuss what we are going to do next and to identify how we take our mini empire up to the next level. I knew the answer already. We needed to build our own porn network, a network that was ready to deal with video as this was inevitably going to hit the online porn industry as soon as broadband hit peoples' homes.

Over the weekend, the plan is set. We are going to spend up to $150,000 and set up our own network. It was going to take six months and over that time I would start finding a buyer to buy the existing porn network I had.

Fast forward to March 2001, things are going well and I have found a potential buyer, but we are delayed. I have spent $25,000 on the domain name sexpass.com and this is going to be our next big thing. As it happened, a few of the staff that worked at Adultcheck.com had left and I had the chance to hire them to work on the new network. We assembled everyone who wanted to move down to Florida. We were working out of an apartment for months, developing and planning. Then we moved some offices ready for the big launch in Boca Raton. This was all happening at the same time I had hit the 'you have made it' phase of my life.

We had some issues with credit card processing companies and getting things just right. I think one of my big failings back then was that I had to have everything perfect. The trouble is, perfection costs time and money.

June hits and I am nearly four times over budget. Looking back, this was ridiculous, but I was obsessed with building the best damn porn site network system in the world.

In May, the sale of my old network of sites with AdultCheck.com went through; I got 20% down and the remainder to be paid over six months. I was genuinely excited.

15th July 2001 - Launch Day. The day we had all be waiting for. It comes and goes and, to be honest, it was fucking disappointing how much support we had. What was wrong? Well, that question was going to be answered in the next few days.

18th July 2001 - Friday evening, The Bahamas, 8.45 p.m. Shit hits the fan. An email comes through from the guy who I sold all my sites to say all of his affiliate accounts were closed down. He wanted to know what was going on and so did I.

I soon started drinking whisky out the bottle.

Now I had various concerns before launch that something wasn't quite right. Everything that we were planning, the guys at Adult Check seemed to be doing something to counter it. My suspicions were so hyped, that I even had our offices professionally swept for bugs and listening devices (they found nothing).

Over the course of the next week, all hell broke loose. I was getting hit hard. Their lawyer was all over me and things were getting shittier day by day.

Basically their owner didn't like that I had hired some of his ex-employees. His fault, he should have kept them if they were that good for him. They were ex-employees, it's not like I poached them! He started accusing me of stealing trade secrets, which was a load of bollocks. In addition to that, he knew I hadn't been fully paid for the old sites I had sold and as far as he was concerned, he was still funding me setting up in competition with him.

I had a grass in my organisation. I know for a fact I did. To this day, I don't know who it was, but I had someone feeding information back to the guys in LA telling them what I was up to. One day, I will find out who it was, not that it matters that much now I guess, but I will find out one day.

After telling his lawyer that I wasn't playing the normal legal games they play, I flew to LA, went to a hotel and am greeted by two big security guards at the door of the meeting room. After being patted down every time I came in and out, I knew these guys were serious. During the course of a two hour meeting, I was told that if it cost a million dollars to make sure I was out of business and not in competition with them, then so be it. Looking back, this was David and Goliath stuff, but I didn't realise it at the time. My fighting spirit came out.

At the same time, the new owner of my old sites said he wasn't paying me the $800,000 he owed me and he wanted his $200,000 back!

I was fucked. I was properly screwed due to another reason, a massive oversight that I didn't think of. I guess my nature is of loyalty, so all the people that said they would promote and support my new system, I really thought they would. But they didn't. Back then some of the top affiliates were making $30,000 - $75,000 a month. What I think happened, (or know really) is that a phone call was made to all of them saying that if they supported me and my new system, then maybe their pay cheques from their current income stream would disappear. Loyalty flies out the window when you are talking mid-five figure earnings each month.

Any business online relies on traffic. Visitors. If you haven't got traffic, you haven't got a business. So there we were, all our biggest affiliates that we were relying on were dead in the water. We truly had a fantastic product, but would have been stuck in a legal battle we couldn't afford.

It's my nature to fight; I think I get it from my dad. It's also my nature to rebel. On the flight back from LA, I thought, "Fuck it! I'm fighting and carrying on!"

As it turns out, I fought too much and tried to carry on way too long. Fighting a losing battle is only hurting one person and it's not the other side who have millions of dollars at their disposal.

The thing is, I was loyal. I had lots of people working for me and I tried my best to keep it going; after all, these guys had moved to Florida to work with me. No matter what I did, I couldn't fight the David and Goliath situation I had gotten myself into.

One Wednesday evening, under the cover of darkness, we packed up the office into a U-haul and everyone parted ways. It was sad, real sad. People went back to their homes, some thousands of miles away, AND I flew back to the islands and that was it. I was done.

I worked with some great and loyal people back then, to name a few, John H, Josh, Gabe, Mike S. Your loyalty still means a lot to me, even to this day.

The next chapter was about to start, but what the hell was I going to do now?

Some 'big hit' this was turning out to be.

The thing with fighting and with business in general is understanding when to give up. I didn't know though.

I had used all my money to keep fighting, nothing I did was working, and it was all turning to shit. People within the industry knew the problems I had and didn't want to touch me. I did find a couple of people to try and work with, but it didn't work. I must mention two people who I still feel guilty towards. Greg D and David VDP. These guys put some money into helping me try and get the network going again (they were big within the industry and didn't care about the people I had problems with).

Remember I said traffic was the problem? Well, it was for the project still, and the game had changed on me. We rebranded the site to xpass.com and tried to relaunch it, but it didn't work and those guys lost some money.

The trouble is when your company is bringing in £150,000 a month, to go and borrow £150,000 doesn't seem a big deal, especially if it means you may be able to survive and get back to the millionaire situation you wanted again. Right? That makes sense. Doesn't it? No.... Remember I said about knowing when to give up? I should have given up a long time before I started borrowing money I hadn't got. Stupidly, I borrowed £150,000 against my parents' house value.

So there was my porn experience, the rise and fall. It was a ride, but the latter part of it I would never want to repeat again. It couldn't get any worse, could it?

> **Marky's Lesson -**
> **Don't think everyone has the same loyalty to you that you may show to them.**
> **Always think of all possibilities.**
> **Worst case scenarios can be far worse. Trust Me.**

Bankruptcy

I t's April 2002. We are back in the UK. The Bahamas was great, but it is not the place I wanted to live when I was struggling financially. The office in Florida had gone, and Kate and I needed the support of our families around us. So we moved back to the UK. We found a great barn conversion to live in, just outside a place called Ashby-de-la-Zouch in Leicestershire.

In true Marky style, I came back and got right on with trying to get something going. I tried loads of things. Not much worked, it was just a case of getting through really.

We had found this great place to live and it was like being on holiday when you came through the gates, but my focus and intent was on getting something to work.

Fast forward to 2003, and Kate is expecting our second child; our son Alexander was born in December.

March 2004 hits and things are tough. I can't keep going much longer. I have this mortgage against my parents' house and the banks were pushing hard against the facilities I had used up.

The thought of bankruptcy was bad. But could I survive? How was I going to turn things around? The answer was, of course, that I wasn't.

When I was faced with the idea that I may have to go bankrupt in 2004, I thought it was the biggest sign of failure ever. But bankruptcy for me was a must. I had tried far too long to keep going and enough was enough. Living back in the UK, trying to find a way to pay my debts, I was overwhelmed. I couldn't believe that all the money was gone. Frankly, I didn't really have a choice but to declare bankruptcy. Filing for bankruptcy in the UK is a little different from in the US, but no matter where you live, bankruptcy feels like failure. It was a whole new low for me and my ego. (Little did I know, moving forward, it was the least of my worries.)

Plus, the vast majority of my debt wasn't just to banks or credit cards. It was to friends and family. So even though through bankruptcy, I was legally forgiven, I was morally obligated to pay that money back. My parents had put up money against their home. I certainly wasn't going to let them lose their house through me!

The day I went bankrupt, in theory I owed no one anything anymore. But morally, as I said, that was a different story. A year later, I was discharged from bankruptcy and the theory is you can start over again with a clean slate, but in my case things were different. So bankruptcy wasn't the magic wand for me that it is for a lot of people.

2004 goes by and with some hard times and hassles, we manage to get through. April 2005, when I am discharged from bankruptcy, I can start again. But, morally, I still have £250,000 of debt to pay off.

My advice: If you are struggling, take professional advice from people who know what they are talking about. I saw it as a sign of massive failure at the time, but that's not the case.

Note: There are a lot of consumer bankruptcies happening now: people who run up consumer debt and just go bankrupt for £20,000, I don't condone this. But business is about risks and to be successful, you have to take risks. Sometimes they don't work out, So there is a big difference in my eyes from a businessman taking risks that eventually don't work, to someone who just wants a load of 'new things' for their house.

> **Marky's Thought -**
> **Most successful multimillionaires have been bankrupt at least once. Do what you have to do, don't fuck any individual or small businessperson over for money if you have to go bankrupt.**
> **But if you have to go, you have to go; you are not helping anyone out by fighting a losing battle.**

Desperate men

It is true that desperate men do desperate things. When you are so desperate to put a situation right, you start considering doing things that you wouldn't normally think of doing. I felt like a rat that was backed into a corner and I didn't know what to do. If I didn't pay this debt off, my parents could lose their house and there is no way I could have that. I owed other people too, people I cared about.

The very worst mindset to have when making decisions is that of desperation. Desperation in all ways changes your mind about things in a very negative way.

Magic wands don't exist but at least give yourself the chance to think about something by standing back from the situation and looking at it from a different viewpoint. It helps. It's something I do all the time now; I get away from things either mentally by meditation or physically by trying to remove myself from a situation to give myself time to think.

Watch the video now!

Debt

Debt is horrible. But there are two types of debt. Good debt and bad debt.

Good debt, I hear you say? Well, yes. Good debt is a debt that you owe but is earning you more than it is costing you. So it could be a mortgage on an investment property that is bringing in rental income and capital growth. If it's putting money in your pocket, it is a good debt. If it is taking money out your pocket monthly, it's bad debt.

Unfortunately, I have had my fair share of bad debt and I know what a bloodsucking demon it can be to cope with.

Debt is evil because:

- Every pound you bring in is instantly minimised in value by its need to contribute to servicing your debt

- It compels you to do things that you would otherwise not do. Debt produces need. Need is completely counter-productive

- It leaves you vulnerable to short-term competitive or marketplace challenges, economic slumps, aberrant events (e.g. 9/11) that you might otherwise painlessly withstand

- It is habit forming. It is easy to get good at juggling debt, comfortable living in debt. You can get so good at survival skills that they are in the way of developing success skills

47

- It is a course of worry, anxiety, and frustration that interferes with wealth attraction, productivity and even physical health

- It lengthens the time required to get to your 'Financial Independence Number', sufficient assets and investment that you never need work to earn another dollar for the rest of your life.

My opinion to debt differs to some of my friends. I don't mind going into debt if it is going to expand my business and, within a short time, put more money into the business.

I have been very silly in the past and gone into debt to just keep fighting. That is foolish, to say the least. There was a fine line in my case between carrying on and breaking through, or going deeper and deeper into debt and still suffering for it all these years on.

Before you go into any debt, ask yourself if it is going to put money in your pocket or take it out. That will answer everything you need to know for you.

Watch the video!

Pot

I never did drugs of any kind, I had no interest, and I don't particularly like alcohol either. It's May 2005 and the financial situation isn't getting any better. I had a guy working with me who was a big pothead, and one night he said he knew how to grow weed.

Remember, desperate men think desperate things.

It got my interest. To cut a long story short, I started growing a few plants in a spare space I had. I learned a lot and.... I was good at growing weed. Needless to say, I started smoking some.

One day, it hits me that if I grew 20 plants in my garage, that could be a few grand if I sold it. I started growing 20 plants in my garage and it went well. For the first time in a few years, as ridiculous as it sounds, I was good at something.

I have always been an all or nothing guy, and in many circumstances, that's a great thing to be, but not always.

I remember having a conversation with a friend of mine at the time, weighing up if I should try and grow weed. Should I just stick with the garage and sell some and pay some monthly bills, or should I find a warehouse and try and grow my way out of debt. As he said to me on that day, "Mark, you know what you are going to do." He was right, I was desperate enough; this debt had become all-consuming. I felt I couldn't really start my life again until I was debt-free.

I made the decision to find a location where I could grow a large amount of plants. I found a warehouse in Leicester. The plan was to grow four lots of plants over 12 months. Get in, get out, pay the debts off and be free again.

Another business I set up while I was trying my hardest to survive was a pawnbrokers shop with a friend of mine. We were selling all kinds of thing on eBay too. We needed a place to store all the eBay stock.

I set up the grow room on the side of the warehouse where I was keeping all the eBay stock. It was a good cover too. It was big, 2,000 square foot. Based on my calculations, I could make £50k - £70k each grow. I didn't know how I was going to sell it, but I figured it was a nice problem to have. Loads of high-quality pot to sell is not going to hang around for too long. I would be able to find people to take it off me. Easy, right?

As always, if I am going to do something, I try and do it the best I can. I read as many books as I could and spent a lot of time on a website called overgrow.com (it's now been taken down by the Canadian government), and I spent hundreds of pounds on books so I could learn the process.

Without wanting to give a lesson here, growing good weed is all about doing it right. It is important to have the right genetics (seeds), the right equipment, the right conditions. I borrowed more money to fund the set up of the grow rooms. The plan was on. We started our first crop in May 2006. I went against the advice of a few people on this. But I felt I needed to do something to sort the situation of my debt out.

The 'grow' went well; the plants were looking good and the room was like a forest. Although I didn't look after the plants myself (someone else did that on a daily basis), I did look after the ones in my garage. To be honest, I really liked it. Nothing to do with the money it could bring in, just the process of growing something from seed that would make you really happy at the end was great. Many a time, I used to chill out in the grow room whilst watering my plants.

Growing a few experimental plants in a garage is a very different thing to growing over 200 in a warehouse in Leicester. The pressure was immense. Anytime I saw a helicopter over the city, I'd shit myself. Helicopters are used to detect heat sources coming from buildings.

I remember one Friday afternoon in June crying in my own car; the pressure of growing so many plants was getting to me.

Maybe I should stop it and just go back to growing in my garage?

My personal thoughts on pot / weed / cannabis

Personally, if you are an adult, I think weed is a better option than alcohol. No, I am not saying smoking is better; smoke of any kind isn't any good for you, but weed as a plant / herb is much better for you in my humble opinion.

I like getting high, I like that I am still in control, but I don't like the 'after feelings' with being drunk and you don't get any hangovers after being high.

I will say, however that having weed before you are 21 years of age is a big no-no in my opinion. The brain isn't full formed until you are 21 and there are way too many kids affected by it in a real, bad way.

There is an argument that weed gives you psychosis, but it's the same risk as someone having their first glass of whisky and becoming an alcoholic in my opinion. Again, these are just my own personal thoughts and in no way am I promoting the mass use of it. But I know one thing. I would rather be in the company of a bunch of stoned people than a bunch of drunken people.

> **Marky's Lesson -**
> **Don't have big eyes and don't let desperation**
> **cloud your judgement.**

The worst day of my life

So there I was working in the pawn shop and running the pot growing space. I was not the person I wanted to be. I had started smoking more marijuana and I was drinking a bit too. The whole situation made me a completely different person. I was so amazingly stressed and I was extremely unhappy.

It was 7th July 2006 and my wife Kate was very unhappy. Something wasn't right. The truth was that nothing was right at that point. She didn't love me anymore and that was the night she left me. I can honestly say, out of all the hard times, this was by far the worst day of my life. I had never had such a heart-wrenching experience. I had gone from being what I thought at the time was happily married with two great boys, to being on my own. As ridiculous as it sounds now, only two days before Kate told me, I had said to my best friend Dawn that although money was a real stress, at least Kate and I were as good as we had ever been. How wrong was I? I was a mess, walking round like a zombie, trying to figure out what had gone so wrong. I was feeling useless. Needless to say, my focus had gone from the warehouse full of weed and the potential cash coming in a few months' time, to my marriage breaking down.

I was consumed by not being with Kate and the boys anymore and I knew something wasn't right. Sure enough, she had started seeing someone else very soon after. When I found out, you can imagine what I was like.

That particular guy didn't work out, but within a few months of leaving, she became involved with what I think at the time was the love of her life, (as she was mine at the time) and she spent the next three years with him.

Divorce

When I said, "I do," to my wife in 2000, I meant it forever. But I'm now old enough to realise life doesn't always work out how you want it. I got divorced from Kate in the following May. A horrible thing. Especially given what else was going on in my life. I used to say to my friends, "It can't get any worst, can it?" Little did I know, yes, it could.

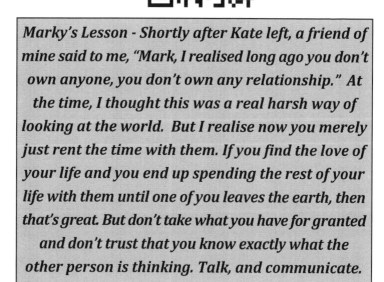

Marky's Lesson - Shortly after Kate left, a friend of mine said to me, "Mark, I realised long ago you don't own anyone, you don't own any relationship." At the time, I thought this was a real harsh way of looking at the world. But I realise now you merely just rent the time with them. If you find the love of your life and you end up spending the rest of your life with them until one of you leaves the earth, then that's great. But don't take what you have for granted and don't trust that you know exactly what the other person is thinking. Talk, and communicate.

Getting Arrested

Little did I know that during this whole time, the warehouse of weed was about to give me even more stress in my life. The summer of 2006 was a hot summer in the UK. What a lot of people don't know is that if pot plants get too hot, they can turn into male plants and this means they produce seeds and not flowers (weed). To counter the rising temperatures, we had to put 12 air conditioning units in the grow rooms.

It's 14th August. I'm going into a lunch meeting with a friend of mine in Leicester and I get a call. "Hi, is this Mark? This is WPC.... and we would like to talk to you. Nothing to worry about, but where are you now?"

Nothing to worry about... I knew instantly it was the grow room. I told them I wasn't around the city and would take a while to get back. I quickly made a call to the shop and it was confirmed I had police there looking for me. Another call to my friend and landlord confirmed they had hit my house too. Full-on 14 policemen and a whole bunch of cars. Something had gone wrong, I had been hit. The worst case scenario had happened.

After four hours of figuring out what was going on and lining up a lawyer to meet me at the police station, I handed myself in.

I was promptly arrested on suspicion of cultivation of cannabis at my garage and the warehouse. What had gone so wrong?

What had happened was that one of the air conditioning units had caught fire on the Sunday. The sprinkler system in the building that I didn't even know was working kicked in and all hell broke loose. A shopkeeper near the back of the building came to work and saw water pouring out the side door. The fire brigade were called, found the second floor full of plants and the police were called. This was on the Sunday. Warrants were put to the court for my arrest and to search all my properties, and I was arrested on the Monday.

If you have never been arrested before, it's not a great thing. The worst part is the police cell. I was arrested at 4 p.m. and let go at 3 p.m. the next day. It was horrible. Not knowing who else, if anyone, they had arrested was bad too. I was initially interviewed by the two arresting officers and, to be honest, they seemed more nervous than I did. My lawyer had advised me to answer, "No comment," to every question. Something that didn't really feel right to be honest, but that's the thing you do when you don't know what is going on.

I can remember pressing the bell for the intercom in the police cell at 9.30 that night asking what was going on and the guy at the end of the line just saying that I was in for the night. My heart sank, one of the worst feelings ever. I counted each brick in the wall that night.

The next morning after hardly any sleep, I was eager to find out what was happening. Who else had they arrested? My mum had called me on my way in to the station the day before, but I didn't say anything; no one could know where I was. Then 10.30 a.m. came and I was told I was going to be interviewed again.

It was just nice to get out the cell, to be honest. I went into a meeting room to be greeted by two older and wiser-looking coppers. One seemed familiar to me. It turned out after I asked him where I knew him from that he had appeared a few times on *Crimewatch* (a UK monthly crime TV programme).

These guys were more serious and more professional than the two rookies that interviewed me the day before. They were part of the financial investigation squad, the people looking at your lifestyle and what you had been doing and earning.

One of their opening lines to me was, "You are a director of a few companies, Mark."

I had to smile when I told them their information was about three years out of date and that I was made bankrupt in 2004, so I was no longer a director of any company. You should have seen their faces drop; they obviously thought they were on to something bigger than it really was. The reality is there hadn't been any cash generated from this operation. I had lost money. At the time, I thought how much bad luck it was that I hadn't managed to get my first grow out the way that was due three weeks later. But, on reflection, the timing was great. If they had caught me three weeks or more later, they would have found £50,000+ of weed and another 300 or so plants in production again. Because by this time, with Kate leaving, I figured I didn't have too much more to lose so I would have carried on growing my way out of debt for sure.

I was kept in for another four hours and finally told I was being police bailed to appear on the 3rd December. The 3rd of December! Why so long? This is your life on hold. And the 3rd December was my youngest son's birthday too.

Upon release, they kept my phone as evidence (there wasn't anything on it as I had wiped it before I handed myself in), so I went to the nearest phone shop and got another phone quick. I needed to know what was going on. First call was to my mum; she was worried and had been trying to get hold of me. The second call was to my shop, and it was confirmed they had pulled my business partner in for questioning too. He was still at the station. I headed right to Kate's house; she had just got another house a few weeks before this had happened and I had called her just before I handed myself in so she knew where I was.

I got to her house and walked down the path and what's the first thing I see? The police officer that had arrested me the day before sitting in Kate's lounge! Fuck me! Can't I get away from these people? Obviously they had wanted to speak to her about my arrest and see if she knew anything. She didn't, of course, and to be honest I was kind of glad they hadn't done any more than interview her at her home.

After waiting for 30 minutes for the officer to leave, I saw Kate. The only thing I was thinking about when I was in that police cell was wanting to be back with her and my boys. After telling her the situation, I told her just that. She said she didn't know what to think.

The reality was she was already seeing someone else but I didn't know at that time.

The next call was back to the house. The police had done a good job of going through it. But to be fair to them, they had taken my dog for a walk twice a day, and they had got the RSPCA out to feed all of the racing pigeons I had just started keeping a few weeks before.

Seriously though, people were mainly concerned for me where I used to live, despite all the hassles I had caused. People's reactions to me were not what I thought they would be. Only one neighbour was funny with me, but even she changed when I started breaking down in tears in front of her.

The next stop was to my mum and dad. This was the thing I wasn't looking forward to. My dad is quite worldly-wise in some wise, but my mum has a very 'all drugs are bad' attitude. I went in and told them what had happened. They were disappointed to say the least, but my dad in his normal spirit was weirdly supportive (he was a police officer back in the day and has a bit of a distain for the police system if he is really honest).

Fast forward a little, and I have to move out of the farm house I was living in and quickly. I packed and sold off what I could and I figured, although I didn't like the area, I would be best to move as close to the boys as possible. So, in September, I moved house.

Being on police bail is hard going if you have never been in trouble before, and in many ways it's as hard as being in prison. Your entire life is on hold, you can't plan anything. I went to my bail appointment in December and it lasted two minutes. All the worry prior to the day was for nothing as they just said they were re-bailing me until April. April! Another four months!

Christmas came and went, and it was horrible. Not because of the police problem too much, but because this was the first Christmas where I hadn't been with the boys or with Kate. I'm not a real fan of Christmas anyway, but being on my own for the first time hurt.

It also hurt because Kate had got a new boyfriend by then and I was a mess. My business partner in the shops also wanted me out of the business. That didn't help either.

My GP put me on medication and I was seeing my secretary which, although was great in some ways, messed my head up even more. When you are sleeping with your secretary but imagining your ex-wife instead, you know things are not right. All I could think about was being with Kate.

Fast forward to April and, you guessed it, the police bailed me again! This time until June.

June's bail appointment came and this time I was charged. The police charged me with two counts of cultivation of cannabis, one for the garage and one for the warehouse, and another count of being in possession of a pepper spray canister.

The stupid thing is, I had cleaned the entire house two weeks before being arrested and had a bunch of boxes still to go through, and the pepper spray was in a box which I brought back a long time ago from the USA where they are completely legal.

So, at this point, I was facing three charges and they interviewed me. They produced a photograph of my dog, Zorba, in the grow room and what appeared to be one of my friends too. Who the fuck had taken a photo in the grow room as it was being set up? The delay ended up being because there was a backlog checking all computers they had seized.

By this time, I'm eating anything I could and drinking brandy like it was water. We finally get a court date and at the last minute, it's moved back by one week. We were going to Crown Court on 23rd October. My lawyer informs me that worst case, I should be looking at getting two to two and a half years' custodial sentence, with a small, very small chance, of a non-custodial sentence. If I'm honest, I knew what was coming. I knew I was going down. But I didn't think it would work out quite as it did.

I never intended for it to be like this, I never intended to be a criminal. I had done something stupid to try and pay my debts off. Where had my millionaire life in the Bahamas gone?

> **Marky's Thought -**
> **There is a fine entrepreneurial line between pushing hard and breaking the law.**

D-Day - court, 23rd October 2007

It's the morning of the court appearance. The night before, I did one of the hardest things I have had to do in my life and that was to say goodbye to my boys not knowing when or if I was going to see them again. I go to the court with my parents, and some of my other family members are there to support me. So too are my other two co-defendants. One was my gardener who looked after the plants and my ex-business partner from the pawn shop who had also been arrested and charged for his connection to the lease of the property.

It was a nervous time waiting, and then I went into the dock. The judge is an unknown entity; my barrister didn't really know him and what he was like. It turned out he wasn't even a full-time judge, he was a recorder, i.e. a barrister that does 5 weeks of judging a year. It seems this guy was out to make a name for himself as a future judge.

Remember, my lawyer Imogen had told me that I was looking to get a maximum of two and a half years and I had pledged guilty, so that took off a third off the sentence.

What was about to happen? Well, what happened was that the judge had made his own mind up before he even saw us in the dock. He didn't listen to any of the mitigating circumstances, none of the reasons why this offence was committed and he gave me four years' custodial sentence. Four fucking years! The other two guys got two and three years.

I can't describe how I felt when he said, "I am giving you the minimum I see fit for this crime.... four years. Send him down." I glanced over at my family to the right of the court room as I went into the next room, another worst time of my life. I sat just behind the door in the next room to hear the fate of my other two co-defendants. Three years and two years. The inexperienced 'judge' forgot to hand me my other two sentences, two years for growing in the garage and a year for the pepper spray.

Giving me four years actually meant it was like a six year sentence, because of the third being knocked off for the guilty plea. I don't think the system is fair. While I was on bail, the sentencing guidelines had been put up. So he was giving me the maximum he could give me the day I was arrested and the maximum sentence was 4 years (two and a half years after the guilty plea).

(I wrote a six-page letter to Judge Godsmark asking why he felt it necessary to give me such a big sentence; he never replied).

I went down to the cells of the court room and I was a shell of a person. I asked the officer if I could change out of my suit into jeans; he let me. My bemused barrister came down to see me; he couldn't figure it out and genuinely was amazed at the sentence term given. He told me I had to be strong for my parents and he would let them know I was ok.

After a lot of pissing around, it was time to leave the court. Little did I know that waiting around was going to be something I needed to get used to.

I was escorted from the court into a prison van; it's the first time I was actually handcuffed. Where was I going? I assumed I was going to Leicester prison. I wasn't; there was no room at the inn. I was going to a local police station for the night. Sitting in that police cell was probably one of the worst nights ever. I was allowed one call. I made that call at 5.30 a.m.; it's the only time the bastards would let me call. Is this what it was going to be like?

The next morning, I'm allowed a shower and then they tell me I'm going to prison. Where am I going, I ask? Doncaster, they tell me. Doncaster! Shit, that's miles away. I wasn't worried for me, but for my family.

PRISONER

VT9828

You are required to have this card on your person at all times. You will be charged £5.00 if you misplace this card.

12-02-08   W1   HMP Sudbury

> *Marky's Thought -*
> *What did I tell you about 'worst case scenarios'*
> *before? Always fear the worst when you are*
> *planning your scenarios. ;)*

Prison

I'm coming out the police cells and I see my other two co-defendants. They look empty. We are all loaded into a prison van. We are on our way to prison. Fuck me, is this really happening?

Next comes one of the worst things about prison for a first-time offender. The prison van. The meat wagon, as I now know it to be called. In the meat wagon, you have individual pens barely enough to fit in and you can see the world outside easily. I was stuck in this 4 x 3 foot box and the world is getting on with its own business out there. I wanted to be out there.

The journey was long. Doncaster is about 130 miles from Leicester. I'm going up the M1 motorway looking out at everyone thinking, "This is hell." We make various stop-offs on the way to pick people up and to drop people off to different establishments. We had some right nutters on board, shouting and swearing to each other between the boxes we were in.

We finally arrived at Doncaster prison. And it's everything you expect it to be. We go through three different gates to get inside. Everything takes so long too.

I am unloaded off the van and placed in another small cell on my own. I am strip-searched and then told to wait in line. This place is full of some weird people. It's noisy and clinical. It's finally my time to go to the desk to get 'checked in'. They ask me a bunch of questions and I'm given my prison number, VT9828. That's me now, prisoner VT9828.

I had packed a few things and they told me what I was and wasn't allowed. The thing I will always remember is that I had 10 pictures of my family and the boys in my bag, but they wouldn't let me take two pictures of the boys in. These two pictures were of them sleeping. I loved to see the boys sleep; they were so cute and peaceful. Anyway, I wasn't allowed to take them into prison, because they hadn't got any T-shirts on whilst sleeping (they had pyjama bottoms on but just not tops).

The prison officer said, "Can't let you have them in here. There are some people in here who would get off on looking at those photos." Fuck me... seriously? This is my life for the next two years.

I then go to another room and I meet a prisoner who is in charge of the first night offenders. He asks me if I have been in before and a bunch of questions, tells me it's not as bad as I think. Yeah right, I think. Then I go to the nurse, who goes through what medication I'm on. At the time, I was on anti-IBS tablets, anti-migraine tablets and a low dose of anti-depressants. I would be given my dosage once a day.

Then I get frogmarched to a small room where we can have some food, because we had missed dinnertime. Then after that, it's the reception wing. This is what you imagine a prison to be like. Doncaster was designed a category A prison, housing the worst offenders. I was a category B prisoner.

Sitting down in the induction wing, an officer tells us various things and then it is time to be shown to my cell. I walk in and this place is bloody horrible, and then it happens; the big door slams shut. That's it; I'm officially a prisoner.

I am sharing with a guy; I can't remember who he was or what he was like but he was ok. The next time the door was opened was at 7:30 a.m.

That's the only time you can get a shower. I thought I would risk it, went and got a shower quickly and saw the other two guys. You have 30 minutes to get your shit together, and then you are locked up again. In a normal 'bang up' prison, you are lucky to have more than an hour in your cell in any 24 hours.

The first few days in Doncaster were hard; it took a few days to get my head around it. We were given emergency phone credit to call. I called my parents and Kate. My mum and dad were coming up to see me on the Saturday.

The only thing you had to do in your cell was watch TV. And weirdly it was a form of connection to the outside word.

Saturday came and it was time for my first visit from my mum and dad. The process of getting from your wing to the visits room was an ordeal in itself. It took about 40 minutes to get through all the security and checks to get to the room. You sit down in a specific chair and wait for your visitors to come. I will never forget the moment my mum and dad walked through the door towards me. They practically had to take over after the initial few minutes of the visit. We all had to get talking about the fallout on the outside of the prison walls. This job would be left to my poor mum and dad to sort out.

There was a lot to sort out, a lot of people to ask about. I had 90 minutes with my mum and dad. It was hard. Much harder though was saying goodbye and going back to the hellhole. I eventually got used to being 'banged up' after a few days; you just cope with it, there isn't any other option. I met with various people in the prison, officers in charge of figuring out where you should go next.

Day 15 of my sentence, and I am told I am moving prison. I was going to a place called Wealstun, an open prison. I pack up all my shit (what little of it there was) and I'm ready. All three of us are in the meat wagon again. On our way to a prison that has two halves, one closed and one open. It was near York.

We arrive at the prison and one side looks like where we have just come from, but the other side doesn't. What was weird though is that you went into the closed side to get processed. I won't ever forget getting off that van, because it was the first time I wasn't handcuffed going anywhere and we were free to move around a bit more within the holding rooms.

This prison had a different feel to it. The only gate on the open side was a normal barrier; you could easily run away if you wanted. It was a head fuck, to be honest. Because once again, you could see the normal world temptingly close. I soon got used to this prison, still not a nice place, but slightly different in feel, slightly more free.

My lawyer had put an appeal in for my sentence, as they thought it was too excessive, so it was just a waiting game. Christmas Eve came and I had a visit from my mum and dad. I had been having visits regularly and it was so nice to see people. When you are in prison, visits are the one thing you look forward to. My poor mum and dad came all the way up to see me on Christmas Eve; it was nice, but at the same time upsetting. Christmas Day came and went and I made the best of it I could. One of the hardest phone calls I had to make was to the boys on Christmas morning. They had been told I was away on business, and that was the way it had to be until I knew how my appeal was going.

The week of Christmas was hard; ok, but hard. I managed to get a job as a cleaner in the prison. I soon figured it was the best thing to do, not that cleaning is my thing normally, but on the inside things were different. Being a cleaner got you your own cell and it meant you could do your work within two hours and in open prisons, if you are fit and healthy, you have to work. So working as a cleaner allowed me to have the day to myself after 11 a.m.

As a cleaner. I earned £7 a week. £1 a day. I used to make £3.50 a minute back in the good old days. Oh, the good old days, where had it all gone wrong?

I placed an order for a £12 stereo; this was my link to the outside world. I was waiting for it to come and it was going to be my saviour over the Christmas week. 24th December came and it had not arrived.

In prison, there are a few people you get on with, and I had got friendly with the guy who ran the library. Jon his name was, and he was from Leicestershire too. One evening, Jon came to my cell door and presented me with a stereo, for me, from nowhere, I had told him about my delay and he had acquired me a stereo for nothing. It was the best Christmas present I have ever had; I had a radio and I had music.

New Year's Eve came and I was due another visit. Mum and Dad came up again; this was hard. Little did I know the day was going to get harder. By this time, I had my own cell on the corner of the wing overlooking the prison gate and people going about their daily lives. At 6 p.m. New Year's Eve, a letter was pushed under my door. It was my appeal notice. It had been refused.

The appeals process in the UK works like this. You first get your appeal sent to a single judge who looks at the case; he can then either deny it or approve it to go to the next stage. The next stage is where three judges look at it and see if the sentence needs to be reduced. Well, I didn't even get to the second stage. The appeal was refused. Why? I don't know, it shouldn't have been. This was my luck the whole way through this thing.

I could have appealed the ruling again, but I ran the risk of a gamble. The gamble being if you appealed it and it got refused again, the judge had the right to restart your sentence, so the few months you had already been in could be wiped out. I was advised to take it on the chin and just get on with it.

New Year's Eve 2007 was a long horrible night, watching people on TV celebrating whilst thinking of everyone on the outside, all my friends and family; it was hard.

The next thing to get over was what I and Kate were going to do with the boys, Now that my appeal had been rejected, I was going to be doing two years in prison. No 'if's and no 'but's.

The open prison wasn't like Doncaster, and there is no way I would have wanted the boys to visit me in there, but Wealstun was different; it wasn't as intimidating. At that moment, they thought I was in the USA working. I had the conversation with Kate about telling them and bringing them to see me. At first, she didn't think it was a good idea, but I said there was no way I wasn't going to see them for at least a year, so eventually we agreed she was going to tell them. The same morning she was going to tell them, we had arranged for her to come up with her mum and bring the boys to visit me. A devastating morning for them, but a free day off school for James.

The boys woke up and Kate told them I was in prison, for a business thing that had gone wrong. I called them up about 8:30 a.m. that morning and the first thing Zandy said to me was, "Daddy, what did you do wrong?"

My heart sank. That afternoon, they came up to see me.

I remember looking out the window which overlooked the car park, eagerly waiting to see them arrive in the car. Sure enough, there they were. My boys. I was going to see them for the first time in three months. I got called over to the visits hall and I walked in. They both ran up to me and gave me a hug, another moment I will never forget. I had two hours with them and it was great. After that, I saw the boys almost every weekend; my mum and dad brought them to visit me.

I got the news that the open side of the prison was closing down and we needed to move. I had a danger of being moved further up north to a place called Kirkam, I couldn't let that happen. I needed to get to Sudbury open prison in Derbyshire. Two weeks went by and I finally got the news I wanted. I was going to Sudbury the next week.

Sudbury prison was only 40 minutes from my family. I got there on the 12th February 2008. My birthday was looking to be a better thing.

My first experience of Sudbury was while waiting to get off the prison van; on entry, this place looked different. Waiting to get off the van, I saw an officer throwing someone's stereo against the wall, because he wasn't allowed it.

I thought, "I hope I don't get him checking me in," but you know it. I got him. Enter Mr O'Brien who was an old school prison officer, 30 years in the job, ex-military who still thought he was in the military. Shouting orders at people. He checked me in and was ok with me, not like the poor guy before. I had somehow built up Sudbury prison to be some holiday camp. Where were the hoola girls and the champagne reception I had invented in my head when I got there? All I got was Mr O'Brien.

I spent 20 months at Sudbury, still working as a cleaner. The place is an old US air force hospital from the mid forties and not much has changed.

I met some interesting people along the way. Many people who were in those places you really didn't want to know or meet. But Sudbury seemed to have more of a diverse group of people. One Sunday evening, I got a knock on my cell door and this big, big guy stood there and said, "Are you Mark?"

I thought, "Who the fuck is this?" It turned out that it was the brother of a friend of my brothers who had been talking on the out and asked Barry to check up on me. Baz became a good friend and did me a few favours which I was really grateful for.

During the 20 months I was there, the population changed so much, as at one time Sudbury catered to your less serious, more white-collar criminal. But over time, with the prison population getting so big, many of the more scumbag side of the population came through a lot quicker than normal. Some people who would have never seen an open prison 10 years ago were now being transferred into open prisons within weeks of being sentenced. I was lucky really; I was deemed a low risk prisoner so got my open status very quickly.

Others I met along the way were not so lucky.

Over a period of time, I got used to prison; you do. I'm not saying for one minute I liked it, but you do get used to your surroundings and make of it what you can. Music played a massive part of my life in prison. Baz helped me secure my music stash and made sure I had enough to listen to. Music has always been a massive part of my life. I used music in there to take me away from being confined. A friend of mine once brought an iPod into prison for me so I could listen to as much music as I wanted. You can get lost in music and it doesn't matter where you are when you listen to it.

In the UK, there is a way that you can start getting day release, if you build up trust and gain the privilege. For me that meant I was eligible for day release after one year. Day release means you leave the prison at, say, 10 a.m. and have to be back by 7 p.m. This was now the thing I was aiming towards. The date in my head was 22nd October 2008. This was the day, in theory, I may be eligible to see the outside world for six hours.

If I was going to make this work for me, I needed to focus on something while in there.

Finding me

During my time on police bail, I ate way too much. Many nights I had too much chocolate, cigars and brandy. I was comfort eating, I guess. So coming into prison, I was a massive 270 lbs in weight.

I had put over 50 lbs on during the year I was on bail. Within two weeks of getting to Wealstun prison, I figured I had better start getting some exercise and using the open grounds, so I start walking and enjoyed very small amounts of jogging. It was hard, real hard. Within two months of getting to Sudbury, I started a proper regime of exercise. As luck would have it, the internal path of Sudbury was dead on 1 km and the path near the fences was a mile long. So I started with the aim of losing as much weight as I could. I had to stop twice on the track during the first week of trying to run a mile, and then got it down to only stopping once, then within a month or so, I was running three miles without stopping. My weight was coming down. I was actually making the best of a bad situation. At the height of my running (some would call it jogging really), I got up to running three miles Monday to Friday, having Saturday off and running 10 miles on a Sunday. For a few weeks towards the end of that regime, I actually missed running if I didn't do it.

I lost over 50 lbs in 10 months. I looked better again, but it wasn't enough. I wanted to look even better so I decided to go to the gym with a friend of mine who was a daily visitor there. During the course of three months, he worked me hard. This was all building up to my first day release. Over the course of three months, I went to the gym four to five times a week and at the end of it, I was in the best physical shape of my life. I looked good and had put some decent muscle mass on. I turned it around.

The other side of finding me was about learning as much as I could; with some much time on my hands, I figured I should read as much as possible. I was lucky that they allowed training materials to be sent in from outside. So I had friends of mine sending me in the latest courses via mail for me to read and watch. My prison cell started to look like its own library. I learned a lot during the 20 months at Sudbury.

The one thing, if I am honest with myself, that I didn't do was to master the art of letting go of my past marriage to Kate. No matter how much I told myself and others I was fine and over it, I wasn't. Prison does weird things to your mind. After all, all you have is time. It still hurt that she wasn't in my life, and although I saw the boys every week, it just wasn't the same. Everything gets polarised in prison. You make things up to be 10 times bigger or worse than they are. It turns out that I needed to meet someone else to finally get over Kate, something that I eventually ended up doing. Although it didn't work out, it finally got me over my divorce.

I had to accept that if I was in this situation, I was going to make the best of it, and I managed to do that. Within 12 months, I was back down to 200lbs and full of muscle and not that much fat. My mind was better too. Although it was still hard and my mind played tricks on me sometimes, I felt ready to take things on again. I had made prison work for me, something that many people just don't bother to do.

Doing time

Despite what the newspapers may say, doing time is hard. No one should comment on it unless they have actually done it. The idea of punishment is that you are removed from society; I get that and I agree with it. But people shouldn't be punished in other ways too. The fact that you are removed from your family is punishment enough.

Personally, I agree that I probably should have been sent to prison for the 'crime'. Although in some states in the USA (the most screwed up prison society in the world), it is legal to grow weed. In no way should it have been for four years to serve two on a first offence. If the judge had given me two years, it would have meant I served about 10 months, as you are eligible to home curfew if you are sentenced to anything under four years. But being that I had got four years, I was not eligible to four months on home detention. Every day that you are in those places matter. During the course of my time at Sudbury, my co-defendants left. Both of them getting 'tagged' or home detention for four months too.

People say cannabis makes you paranoid. Well during the time I was in prison, I had no cannabis and I can tell you prison makes you more paranoid than anything else I have had or experienced.

There is a certain mentality in prison, one of fear, one of paranoia. Everything is privilege and permission-based and if you screw up, or the screws (guards) think you have screwed up, you are looking at losing out in some way.

I had my fair share of setbacks in prison too. The 22nd of October was coming nearer and nearer now, and I was getting excited. As part of the privilege scheme, you get randomly drug tested every three weeks in prison. I volunteered for them. Drugs are a massive problem in prison and drug testing is part of the privilege system that allows you to get on inside. I had been drug tested voluntarily for months prior to the planned first day release I was going to be allowed to have. But every prisoner before day release gets a compulsory drugs test which gets sent off to a lab in London for in-depth testing. I thought nothing of it when I was called up for mine, but a week later, devastation hit.

It's 7.30 a.m., the Thursday before my first planned day release on the Saturday. The day I had been waiting for, for a whole year. My name gets called up over the tannoy to go to the cells. The cells is the place you don't want to be called to go to. That's the segregation block. If you are in there, it means you are in trouble in some way. I go along and get given papers. The papers demanded I go before a prison governor at 10.30 a.m. that day. Why? Because my drugs test had come back positive for ecstasy. Ecstasy! I don't even know what ecstasy looks like, never mind have ever had any.

I only had three hours to figure out what the hell was going on, so I go to health care and ask them. They tell me there is a chance that some of the prescription medication I was on could show up as a false positive on a drugs test. Here is the deal. When you go for this drugs test, they take two samples from you and they also ask you to say if you are taking any medication, which I was. I signed to say that I was and that they had permission to speak to the in-house prison doctors if need be.

So at the hearing before the governor, I explained what I had found out at health care and that it was vitally important I still be allowed out on my day release because my two children had been looking forward to this day for months and months. I asked that I would be allowed out still pending the second test that is made. I also pointed out that I had months and months of random voluntary drugs tests which had all been negative. No dice. They insisted they had to wait until the second test came back and there was a chance that the test wouldn't be back anytime soon, especially not before Saturday morning. I was gutted. I went and found the head governor, but she was no help. I had to tell the boys I wasn't coming out.

The following Friday was the morning I got the news that the second drugs test had come back as a false positive against the medication I was on. And I was allowed out on the Saturday. Finally.

It was the best feeling leaving those gates, even if it was only for six short hours.

The system in there is messed up; they don't automatically do another second drugs test on the second sample. They send back the positive and then wait to request another one if need be. This screws people's lives up, and isn't fair, especially as I had done nothing wrong. It turns out the anti-migraine tablets I was taking every day showed up as a false positive on the drugs test. How's your luck, eh?

My first six hour day release was great, although slightly weird. Being free for the first time in a year, and seeing the outside was amazing. I don't know how people who have been locked up a long, long time cope.

There were various other setback and ups and down in prison, but the other main event was about to come.

Remember, I said the mentality is different in prison; people don't act how they normally would on the outside? The drugs problem was bad too. The thing is, you may read this and think that's a bit weird for someone in on a cannabis charge to say, but it's different.

First of all, I have never, nor ever will try any other type of drug other than weed. I have no interest in anything that is man-made. Secondly, you are in an open prison, so things in some ways are more open to problems than a closed jail where you are behind a door for up to 23 hours a day. It would be easy for someone else to throw something in your cell and then your cell be searched and for you to get in trouble. No word of a lie, you could walk down some of the wings at night and get high just from having a walk. And I didn't like it. Fortunately, I was lucky enough to be moved to a wing on the outer perimeter of the prison, the Hilton wing if you will, full of more established, 'nicer' prisoners. They didn't have any kind of problems.

Pissing off the wrong people is something you should try not to do in prison. But I managed to do it. Someone had overheard me saying how ridiculous the drug problem was in there and that had got back to one of the heads of the two drugs gangs in the jail. In addition to that, one of the officers thought it would be good to move me from my nice single cell to the roughest hardest, drug-riddled wing in the prison.

Stan

Enter Stan. I first met Stuart (or Stan, as his friends call him) the very first night I got to Sudbury prison. He was sharing a cell with my co-defendant, who had already got to the prison a month before me. My first impression of him as I walked around the path in the grounds was of a big 6 foot four inch guy who was one of the only few people to make me feel small and he looked as hard as nails. But at the same time he was most friendly to me and made me feel welcome. Even asking me if I needed anything on my first night and lending me some soap. (Don't laugh; things that you wouldn't take for granted in the normal outside world are in short supply in prison.)

Over the course of the coming months, Stan and I became great friends. In theory, the friendship should never have worked. I wasn't a real criminal in the eyes of the general prison population; I was just a guy that got caught growing weed. Stan, however, was a career criminal. If you met him without knowing him, he could give off an intimidating persona, but once you got to know him, he was far from that. Not that many people got to know him properly. In prison, you say hello to a lot of people, but you don't really know them.

I spent pretty much every day in the presence of Stan, and was lucky enough to have a cell next door to him at one point. Stan was doing a 14 year sentence for the importation of cannabis. His car was bugged by the police and he got stitched up by a bunch of people he worked with. Something I learned about people like Stan is that they are very smart people. Now you may read this and say, "Well he's not that smart - he got caught!" but I learned one thing. It's always other people that let them down. For every one person you have in your organisation, you have another potential weakness. It's the same in any entrepreneurial sphere. Many times, other people are your weakest link to success. When the shit hit the fan, people started squealing and those so-called friends of Stan's sent him down a big river without any paddles.

Stan got some hassle from others for being such good friends with me. In many people's eyes, I was or could have been, a grass. This was because I didn't actually fit into the regime and the type of people who were in there. Stan taught me to play chess; he was a master chess player and regularly played many games 'inter prison'. How can you play a game of chess between different prisons, I hear you ask? Well, you write down your move by letter and send it to your competition somewhere in another jail in the world and he sends you his move back. Stan was in the top 10 of the UK prison chess population. Like I say, a very smart guy. I never did beat him at chess but would like to think that one day I will ;)

We walked miles and miles and talked about everything you could imagine, from great ideas that could make us our fortunes when we got out, to love and girls. In many ways, we were very similar when it came to love and girls. Stan had fallen in love big time with a girl he had never kissed. She was younger than him and had worked at a local coffee shop. He was close to getting her to come on a date with him once, but then he got arrested and that all went away quickly. During my prison time, I would be lying if I said I wasn't still deeply in love with Kate. Or at least, I thought I was. But at the same time, I was aware nothing was ever going to happen and I needed to find a new love of my life.

Stan thought he had met the love of his life; let's call her Annabelle for the purposes of this book. Annabelle was someone he hadn't spoken to for four years by the time I met him and, for various reasons, he wasn't going to be eligible for day release like I was. I was given the job of trying to find out where she was living and to get in touch with her. I tracked her down on one of my day releases. She was living and working in Barcelona. The plan was hatched that I was going to email her and ask her if Stan could write to her. She didn't respond, but it was possible she didn't get the email. My next plan was to call and ask if we could have a work email for her as the company she works for looked really big, I was sure the receptionist would give me her work email address. I called the office in Barcelona one day and the conversation went something like this:

- "Hi, can I have Annabelle's email address please as I would like to send her an email?"

- "Who is this?"

- "My name is Mark and I need to send Annabelle an email but I have lost her email."

- "Is this personal or business?"

- "It's personal."

- "Well, this is Annabella"

I had been rumbled. I didn't know what to say. I said what I was really calling for and the conversation ended quickly. I then messaged her on Facebook, but nothing ever happened. Poor Stan, I did, however, smuggle a picture of her from her Facebook page back in for him to see. You have never seen a man like he was when he saw it, I remember one night standing with him looking up at the stars trying to figure out where Barcelona was and whether she could see the same star as us. Soppy bastards, the both of us. This was the other side of Stan very few people saw. He had ended up being my best friend in prison and still to this day is one of my best friends and will be for life. Although he lives far away from me, we still love each other like brothers.

Back to my last big problem in prison. I was moved onto one of the most horrible wings and this place was bad and populated by members of one of the drug gangs. The same drug gang I had inadvertently pissed off by saying the amount of drug use in the jail was ridiculous, and the screws were telling me to move over there! The bastards!

I get my marching orders to get off the Hilton wing and to go to Wing E7. This place was bad. I told Stan what was happening. He and I were living next to each other on the Hilton wing at the time and he said, "I think I'd better help you move over there, Mark." We both walked onto the wing, and, for me, it was like the scene out of *The Green Mile*, walking on death row, but I didn't need to worry at that time because I was with Stan. Stan wasn't afraid of anyone, people respected him too. He helped me move all my stuff in to my 'new house'. Fortunately, I shared a cell with a guy called Justin, who was a decent armed robber, a young lad who just wanted to get out and be with his new child. I do hope he is still out and on the straight and narrow. (Even he got hassle from people because he was friendly to me.)

I moved all my stuff on to the wing and I tried to make sure I was seen as much as I can be with Stan. I spent five weeks on that wing, the worst time of my sentence really. Always looking over my shoulder, I was not happy at all. There was a possibility of moving onto another wing to fill a bed of someone I knew who was getting out soon, but would I get the move? Would I be allowed? I had a few weeks to survive until I would know for sure.

One particular day, the word around the prison was that this gang were getting more and more wary of me and thought I was a plant, a grass, a wrong 'un. Combine this with the chattering of my opinions about the drugs issue in the jail and I was a marked man. Over the space of a few days, it got to where I was only ever with a few of my friends or in my cell.

Things were getting so bad. I was genuinely worried that I was going to get done over. Now I am a big enough guy to not be intimidated by most people but it's different in prison. It's hard and I'm not even a proper criminal. One particular night, Stan tells me that tension is building and he has heard rumours that I might get done over. So much so, that he needed to step in, or I was going to get done over good an' proper.

Stan went to see the head of the gang telling him that if anything happened to me, they would have Stan to deal with. I woke up the next morning and it was like a different feeling. Word had gotten around that I wasn't to be touched, or else. Stan had saved me big time, and in doing so, had put his reputation on the line. People still thought I was a grass and for someone like Stan to stick up for me was a big gesture. Like I say, on paper, he and I shouldn't have been friends as we were two very different people in most people's eyes. Not many people saw the connection that we had.

From that week onwards, the prison was a different place to live. I got my move to another very quiet wing with a friend of mine, which is where I spent my last six months of my sentence. Stan's family were all in Norwich and he got the chance to be moved to a small open section of Norwich prison. It was a sad day for me the day he left; he was really the only friend I had, as everyone else had been discharged. But it meant he was able to see more of his family and by this time, I was doing volunteering work outside the prison five days a week so didn't see that much of him.

Stan got out in May 2010; this is a picture of us when I visited him in Norwich once he was finally released.

He and I are still the best of friends and we speak and see each other as much as we can; I would do anything for him and he would me. You can't buy friendship like that, no matter what your background or public perception. Everyone has two sides to them. Sometimes you just need to get to know people a little first to see it. I truly love the guy as a friend and imagine us as lifelong friends, no matter what.

Finishing my time

I was getting towards the end of my time. I had four months left; I was to be released on the 22nd October 2009. I swear the weeks, days and hours went much slower during those last four months. As part of the privilege earned, I was allowed out overnight to get me used to being back in the outside world. Resettlement, they called it.

The officers were split into three types. Horrible bastards that would do anything to fuck your life up, non-descript officers who were a nothingness to you, and then there were a few genuinely friendly and nice officers. Spencer and Moffat were two of the good officers. There was one other officer who was a nice guy getting ready to retire. I can't remember his name but I can remember inviting him into my cell for a cup of tea at 2 a.m. when I was awake and he was doing his nightly checks. A nice guy with a sad story to tell in life himself. I do hope he is living a happy retirement now.

Just like a bad smell, Mr O'Brien, the first officer I had experienced on my arrival to Sudbury, was still there. But, you know what, I had grown to like the old timer. No one could get rid of him though; even the governor had tried once or twice. But as he once told me, prison officers are some of the hardest people to fire! :) I had started to like O'Brien during my 20 months and I had realised something about him. If he thought you were a dickhead, he would treat you like a dickhead. If he thought you were ok and decent, he was decent back to you. We had a few laughs together, especially when the rumour was going around the jail that I had been caught taking speed. He regularly used to catch me running and shout, "Hello, speedy," at the top of his voice.

I met some people in prison who should never ever have been in. Some sad cases too. One particular man who always comes to mind was someone called George. George was a 72-year-old man, who one day had gone out for fish and chips for him and his wife. He was going across country and turned right into a lane and a bike, which was proven to have been going too fast, came over the brow of a hill and hit into George's car. The motorbike driver died. Now, of course, I feel sorry for anyone whose family member has died, but George hadn't done anything wrong. He hadn't been on a mobile phone or anything, it was just an accident caused by the bike going too fast. George was sentenced to 12 months. Serving six months. That's just wrong. He should have never been sent to prison. Take the guy's driving license off him or never let him drive again, but don't send him to prison. The guy had never done anything wrong in his life; he came into prison at nine stone and left at seven stone. His wife was that worried about him, she called the governor up about him and his health. This UK 'justice' system is full of shit.

I met a few sad cases in prison, some people with nowhere to go or to live on their release. I know of people who committed suicide within days of release from prison. For whatever reason, they couldn't face life, or life on the out.

My last night in prison came. The last night I had been waiting for. I said goodbye to the few people I knew still, and went to sleep for the very last time as a prisoner. I woke up early the next day and went to the check-out reception. Who was there checking me out? Mr O'Brien, the same guy I had met 20 months before checking me in.

I left prison at 8.30 a.m. on the 22nd October 2009. My life was about to start again.

My Lessons and Thoughts on Prison:

- Prison doesn't really work for the people it is supposed to.

- I was sent to prison for two years, a massive waste to me and to the government who sent me there. Two months would have been enough of a lesson to me.

- Some people don't have any quality of life outside of prison, and it's better for them inside. Those are the people that need help to make sure their lives are better when released.

- 70% of people come back to prison. What the fuck is that all about? It shows you something isn't working.

- Prison is hard; don't listen to what you hear about it being like a holiday camp. It's hard. No one should comment on 'the cushy life' that prisoners have unless they have done it themselves.

- Prison changes you; it changed me in many ways, far too many changes to list here.

- Prison makes you appreciate things I never thought I would appreciate before I experienced it. Fish and chips and cuddles from your family, to name just a few.

- Why anyone would want to go back to those places is beyond me.

Marky's Thought -
Unless you have done time, you have no right to have a negative opinion about it.
All those newspapers are talking about prisoners having an easy life, and they have not got a clue.
I challenge anyone to do a month in prison and then say it's easy.

Freedom

I have my freedom back! This is me. I had just got out, a free man again, and the fun really started to begin. When you are in prison, you think everything is going to be great when you get out, all flowers and bells. Well, it's not quite like that. You have lost some 'friends' along the way and you have come out to a different place than when you went in.

The day I got out, I launched my first blog:

10:30 a.m., Millionaire Challenge launched. It was a daily blog about how I was going to get my life back on track and start earning my millions back. It would be easy, right?

Many people don't know that you have to visit a probation officer for the remainder of your time on licence; in my case, it was two more years. If they or the police think you have done anything wrong, they can send you back to prison to serve the rest of your time. So in many ways, the paranoia continued.

So here I am; 34, divorced with two kids, and not a pot to piss in. I had £100 to my name and was £40,000 deeper in debt due to all the interest that had accumulated while I was away. I needed to work quickly. I need to get my life back. The Bahamas and the life I had back then felt like a long time in the past. Freedom was great, but in many ways, the pressure of life and all it brings hits you like a ton of brick.

I had my freedom, but the two years on licence were harder than I thought.

A criminal record means you have limitations on what you can do. I can never use a gun again (not that it bothers me); in theory, I am never allowed to buy fireworks again either, screwed up, hey? Also, another limitation you have on you after you have done your time is that you are unable to travel to the US and many other countries; I feel this is wrong. You do your time so you should be free. If you are a terrorist or a potential danger to people, then that is different. But I think it's screwed up that I can't fly into LAX, California, a place where weed is almost legal to use anyway, and why can't I fly into LA? Because the American government see me as a big time criminal who grows weed. That's seriously messed up.

My first real taste of freedom without anyone looking over my shoulder came on my first overseas trip in four years. It was to Cyprus. On the plane, I remember smiling and thinking, "Thank fuck that chapter of my life is over."

Onwards and upwards!

> ## Marky's Thought -
> ### Freedom is the most precious thing you have in your life today.

*"Although no one
can go back
and make
a brand new start,
anyone can start from now
and make a
brand new ending."*

Carl Bard

Starting Again

S tarting again was hard. Far harder than I thought it was going to be. The first few months were a challenge, to say the least. Like I have said before, when you are in prison doing time you somehow invent the story in your head that life is going to be all great. You think that nothing is going to get in the way because you have your freedom back and that means you can do anything.

The reality is far from the truth though.

I left prison deeper in debt than when I went in, and without the debt around me, things would have been very different.

For the first 10 months, I found myself living back at my parents; I had no choice. Not something you want to be doing at 34, with two kids and the memory of the kind of life you had before it all kicked off.

Looking back, it took me a few months to really get my head straight. I hooked up with a girl I had known before and we had an arrangement, so that made things better, but in many ways it was the hardest time.

I had so much ambition to get things going again and the two years I had experienced made me want it even more. I had been in contact with Brad Gosse, my friend who I had known all those years before from the adult industry days.

He had gone on to set up a successful Internet marketing business so during my day releases from prison, the plan was that I would start my business the week after I got out. After a few briefing calls, the plan was set. I needed to do a product online that didn't cost me any money to set up. Eventually Brad came up with the idea of my producing royalty-free music tracks using GarageBand on my Mac; it was free and all it would cost me was my time.

I spent a few days learning GarageBand and getting the tracks done. I created 30 royalty-free music tracks. Brad helped me to put a sales page together and we launched it at 3 a.m. in the morning. Just 15 minutes later, I had my first sale from the WarriorForum.

Now I was broke, broker than broke, so much so that Brad had to PayPal my $20 to list my advert on the forum. That product went on to gross a few thousand dollars. Funnily enough, Brad and I have just done another music product offering over 270 tracks and we sold the entire site a month after launch for decent money. Full circle. :)

I was in business again and started producing as many products as I could so as to get some money coming in. I started networking and I had to use my back story to get noticed. Normally I am not one for shouting about things, and back in the adult industry days, no one knew who I was for month after month, but this was different. If I didn't mention my past, people would call me out on it, so I had to use it to my advantage, and use it I did. I even had people on the forum doubt that the story was real.

It was real enough!

Within the first 12 months, I had made a good start. Nowhere near good enough for me at the time, but looking back I was making the best I could of the situation I was in. I reconnected with Simon Hodgkinson in the February of 2010 at an event in Newcastle. I explained what had been going on and why he hadn't heard from me (I had actually sent Simon a letter from Doncaster prison explaining where I had gone, but he never got it, arsehole screws). The letter was written because I had hit Simon and Jeremy, his business partner, with a business idea at a networking event that I went to, two weeks before I got sent down. Simon went on to help and advise me too.

You meet some nice people along the way. I owe Brad a great deal; he and I both started in the adult industry at the same time and for much of the time my companies were earning far more than his, but here's the thing. He was sensible, diversified and kept all his money.

Brad, many thanks for your support, even during the times when some people may have doubted whether you should have been supporting me. (Funnily enough, the publicity Brad got from helping me out and helping me to achieve the results I got in the first year helped him massively.) He developed a big following, got many coaching clients and got known as a result. Win/win situations are always the best.

It was not an easy ride, but at least I was back in the game.

Depression

Until you have had it, you don't really know what it's like. I think I first got it in 2007. I don't claim to fully understand depression but I have much more of a handle on it than I used to. Nothing can prepare you for how it grips you.

I think this quote from Stephen Fry sums it up pretty well.

"If you know someone who's depressed, please resolve never to ask them why.

Depression isn't a straightforward response to a bad situation; depression just is, like the weather. Try to understand the blackness, lethargy, hopelessness and loneliness they're going through.

Be there for them when they come through the other side. It's hard to be a friend to someone who's depressed, but it is one of the kindest, noblest, and best things you will ever do."

Stephen Fry

This is a post I made in March 2013 about my battle with depression. It was the first time I ever spoke about it publicly:

The phoenix – the reality of depression for me

It was 3 p.m. on 14th February 2013. I'm in bed. I've been in bed on and off for two days now. My kids have just left. I'm broken. I'm done in. I'm ill.

I've been totally useless to my kids over the last 24 hours; they looked after me really. I didn't have to see them how I was; I probably shouldn't have had them. At that time, however, a hug from them was just about the only thing that made me feel anything.

I'm a mess. I was driving yesterday and had a pain in my right side of my head, like someone had hit me hard, followed by blurred vision travelling across my eyes from right to left. I know it was a migraine, but it scared me.

I can't believe I just let my boys or my ex-wife see me in such a state, but having a few cuddles with the boys helped me a little. It also reminded me why I can't give up. I've been up and down for weeks now; stressed, being ok, putting a brave face on, getting on with it etc.

My grandfather died on Sunday. To be honest, it was expected, but it still hurt. Most people think I have taken the death of my grandfather four days ago harder than expected. There has been a bunch of other stuff going on that is not worth talking about, but needless to say, I feel like I'm done.

Staring at the dark room, I feel ill, and I feel empty. Up until this point, I have got back into exercising for a decent few days and have been trying my best, but it's all come crashing down. Oh, and when I am like this, I comfort eat when I don't have migraines; migraines make me not eat. Normally, I comfort eat though.

I have never had suicidal thoughts – my two boys and my loving and supportive family mean that hasn't happened.

But I do feel like giving up and with different circumstances, I can see why some people feel suicidal. If you don't feel like you have people around you who need you, it could happen, I guess.

The reality is, I feel fucked.

I'm writing this now on 27th February and I have had intermittent headaches since. Nothing I do seem to help with the headaches or tension. It's a vicious circle.

I'm writing this now because I need to do something and I've slept so much over the last two weeks that I can't sleep anymore.

This is one of the hardest battles I've had to deal with. It's so hard to describe. Maybe for someone who lives the life I do, with massive highs and lows, it's to be expected. I have led a life in my earlier years that some people can only dream of living. I've been lucky; maybe that's the problem, maybe once you have had what I had and lost it, it's 10 times harder.

The highs and the lows are ridiculous. I don't understand it, I don't want it.

I met with my doctor two days ago. I'm on three times the medication I was on when I first started. Three times the dosage to what I was on whilst in prison. What the fuck is that all about? :-(

I actually made my doctor laugh when he first asked me the question, "What has contributed to you feeling like this and what will make you feel better?"

I told him it's nothing that a good woman and a couple of hundred grand wouldn't fix. :)

In reality, it's more than this.

So, what's happening to make me feel like this?

Summary – The Story So Far

I have been through a lot in the last few years (and before I start, I'm not telling you this for you to feel sorry for me). Many of the things that have happened to me have been my own stupid fault. I am only telling you to set the context of what has been going on in my life.

Twelve years ago, I was a millionaire at 25 sitting on a beach in The Bahamas with my wife and child. I was living a life most people could only dream of. Then, in 2001, I lost the lot – millions pretty much gone in months. I came back to the UK in 2002, battled to keep going and eventually had no choice but to go bankrupt. This, at the time, was just about the worst time of life; bankruptcy, to me, was the ultimate sign of failure. Little did I know it was nothing compared to what I had in store in the coming years.

Fast forward to 2006 – my wife and I have had another child, financial pressure is still tough, very tough. Why, you may ask, if you were made bankrupt in 2004? Surely all of your debt was wiped? In theory, yes, but morally, no. Some of my biggest creditors were friends and family. My family are normal working people, but in the good times I loaned money against the family home to keep going. Stupid now, I know, but at the time I thought it was the best thing to do. So, even though I was discharged of all my debts, there was no way I could not pay back my parents and other friends I owed money to.

It's now 2005 and I'm feeling backed into a corner. These debts are killing me in my mind. How the fuck am I going to get them paid back? I've made some pretty stupid decisions in my time, but the next 'solution' to become debt-free has to be at the top of the list. Before we get into that though, in July 2006, my wife of six years, whom I had two boys with, told me she didn't love me like she should and was leaving me. The worst thing that could ever happen to me just had... or had it?

Spending my days in a total daze was a living nightmare. However, the nightmare was due to get worst. On 14th August 2006, I got arrested for growing cannabis. I spent 14 months on police bail and then, in October 2007, got sentenced to four years in prison. It was horrible. That's not something I will go into here. I got released in October 2009 and started again.

I have to say that the depression I have suffered in the last year or so gives all of the above a good run for its money.

So where am I now?

Well, I'm a Z-list Internet Marketer who is completely disillusioned with the bullshit market I find myself in. I've stopped everything in my business and I'm planning to start over again with a new plan using what I have built up and the knowledge I've got.

The reality of the business side of my business is that I am nowhere near where I want to be in my business life. Nowhere. By now I thought I would have a sustainable long-term business, but the reality is I've had so many hits in the last 18 months, I'm beat.

It's time to start again and make some big changes.

In my personal side of things, I've been single for six and a half years... I know, it's a long time. The reality of this is that two of those years were spent at Her Majesty's pleasure, and I have had various 'happenings' with women over the six years or so. In the recent three to four months, I've turned down a few women and dates with them. I did meet one woman who changed my mind about love and relationships again, but that didn't work out for reasons I won't go into here. The only good thing about the short time I was with her was that she made me realise I could love again, and to be honest once and for all, finally got me over my ex-wife.

The trouble with prison life is that if you hear of your ex-missus going out with her new boyfriend for a coffee, sitting on the bed in your prison cell for hours a day seems to polarise everything and you end up imagining the two of them drinking pink champagne and having wild sex.

So, if I'm honest, the only woman I have felt I could spend the rest of my life with and love since my ex-wife has made me more miserable in the past eight months and probably added a great deal to my current depressive state. But I think about her now instead of my ex-wife, which actually is better for me, I guess.

This depression is hard, because it makes me question what I've got to offer a woman. I know when I'm better that I have a lot – I'm loving, caring and very loyal – but that little thing in my mind tells me otherwise when I'm like this.

So although I have some great friends and family around me, being single for so long creates a great deal of loneliness. It's screwed up though because I really can't be bothered to go out and date or meet anyone, so I shouldn't moan about that, I guess. I know I still think about the person I shouldn't, and all my friends and family tell me to move on and find someone else. I'm a complicated guy when it comes to relationships. I don't find that many women attractive. Relationships and me is a whole other book, so I better not carry on.

But yeah, nothing a good woman and a few hundred grand won't sort out, right? :)

It's bloody hard to explain to people who have experienced depression, let alone someone who has been lucky enough not to have suffered from this bloody illness.

And you know what? It is an illness. The first time I ever properly acknowledged it as an illness was after I read Stan Collymore's tweet about his battle with depression. I actually read his tweet about two hours after he published it; I was up in the early hours of the morning and everything he said resonated with me. Actually, after reading what Stan said, I used the word depression for the first time. Previously, I guess I had been embarrassed.

Publicly, I'm a strong, resilient guy and most of the time I am, but when I get gripped by this, I feel like the weakest man to have ever lived.

How can someone as seemingly strong as me be depressed?

My life has been very public, my entire past is documented online and I have already tried to be as open and honest with people as possible (perhaps to my detriment sometimes). But this is one of the few things I have never talked about publicly. Like I say, getting through to myself that this is an illness and not just being 'weak' has been a long road, but I think it's just about hitting me what I'm really dealing with.

Why have I written about this? It's time to be honest with myself, and it's time to be honest with people that know me, I guess. Also, if it helps just one person who is going through the same things but who has not said anything to anyone yet, then it's worth it.

The risk is that some people will take advantage of me, perhaps even mock me for writing this. There are a fair few people that will hate the day when I am a raging success again and love it that I'm struggling. But, to be honest, I don't care anymore. I am me and this is part of me now.

If I was going to give up, I would have done it by now. During my good times, nothing will stop me getting the life back that I want. I urge you to speak to people if you are suffering. Like I say, it's hard to understand, but there are people that can help.

Will the phoenix rise from the ashes again? You bet your fucking life it will... I'm just not sure when.

When I read back through this passage, I can still remember how it felt, and nothing at the time made any difference. I think it's very easy for entrepreneurs to suffer from depression. We are our own worst critics and we set the standard high for ourselves. I think the highs and lows of my life have taken their toll. One of the biggest things I can't figure out is how quickly things can change. One minute, you can be great, and the next hour, you can dip and have no real explanation for it. I feel confident over time that my depression will get easier and easier. I think it won't hit me as hard when I am somewhere back where I want to be in life. A loving decent woman and me sitting in my lounge on my hill should help a great deal. ;)

Days like today as I am writing this book, I feel great about my life. I'm excited for the future, both personally and business-wise. I'm looking forward to meeting the new love of my life, I'm also looking forward to two exciting new businesses that I am involved and for them to become successful. But, I now realise things can change quickly. It's about dealing with it and one day the amount of 'bad days' I have will be virtually non-existent because my life will so fucking great. ;)

I don't want to write any more about depression in this book; I have acknowledged the issue but I don't want to make anyone feel down by reading my book, but at the same time, this book is all about being real and depression has been a very real thing in my life. No matter how much I try and understand it, I don't want it in my life. I hate that I have it, I don't want to feel like I do something. But no matter what, feeling empty, dead inside and a shell of my former self is something that I have got used to happening every now and then.

> ***Marky's Thought -***
> ***If you are suffering from depression, don't suffer in silence, there is help out there. One of the things I have learned over the last few years is that depression is not a weakness; it's an illness that needs to be treated and dealt with like any other physical illness would be.***

*"Look after yourself,
there is only one you.
One life,
make the most of it.*

*This is not
a rehearsal."*

Looking After Number One

Look after number one. Sounds quite selfish, doesn't it? Saying that you should look after yourself first before you take care of anyone else and it's something I have not been very good at in the past. I'm still not great at it sometimes now. But you learn, you learn that you have to.

I have a paradox in my life really. I don't care what many people think about me, my life or any aspect of it. But there are a few people in my life where I do care deeply about what they think of me. I also have a massive amount of loyalty to those people, including work colleagues, friends and family. Guilt of mistakes from the past, especially regarding my friends and family and the debts I built up, caused a massive problem for me. In a non-monetary sense, it's a problem too sometimes.

I have learned though. I have learned that most people will always look after themselves first. And it's something over the last few years I have tried to do myself. And I have managed it to some degree. The way I managed to do it was by telling myself that I was of no use to the people I really cared about if I was a mess, running on half stressed and depressed etc. This then caused me to look after number one in some situations where I previously wouldn't have done.

I have never been any good at managing people. I am either too soft and they get away with anything, or I am too hard and they end up leaving when I don't want them to.

A cynic may say that this attitude of looking after number one breeds selfishness and a society where there is no love in the world. But I know I am too soft and have been way too generous in my past; in fact, to the detriment of me and my family. I also know that people don't treat me with the same respect and loyalty as I feel they should. Like I have said, I am a naturally trusting person; I like to believe in people and they are honest. I have learned, sadly, that's not always the case.

So my advice to you is, without becoming a 'Gordon Gecko type greed is good' character in life and in business, you MUST look after yourself first, physically, mentality, financially. In all ways. This way, you are in a better situation to care for the people that really matter to you.

Saying 'Fuck You'

Sometimes you just have to say 'Fuck You' to a situation or people. I'm not naturally an angry person, nor do I particularly like hassles, but sometimes people just take the piss. Saying 'Fuck You' to a situation or a person, either directly or in your head, is the best way of looking after yourself, your mind and not getting hurt. Don't let people walk all over you. I have done this a few times in the last two years and I am better for it. See my bit further on in the book about FU Motivation too.

Fuck It

I read a great book by a guy called John C Parkin called *F**k It*. You should too. It's not an aggressive book in any way, but it helps you to think slightly differently and to live your life in a more carefree way. Saying 'Fuck It' to any situation and not worrying about things is a tremendously powerful tool. I won't try and duplicate what John has done in his book; you should just read the book sometime.

Until then, try saying 'Fuck It' to situations that come up in your life.

I have done it; I have spent an entire week of trying it. I had a particularly bad time caused by a situation and an ex-girlfriend who I was hurt by and just couldn't stop thinking about, then it turned to depression. But, you know what? Whenever I thought about the situation, I just smiled and said, "Fuck it." I normally followed on by saying something positive to myself and it worked.

Try it. Fuck what people think, what you think you should do or say. Fuck it. It's a powerful thing, trust me.

Giving up?

Have you ever felt like giving up? I have so many times in the last seven years. Many people have said to me that they would have given up if they were me in the past. But what are you going to do?

Don't get me wrong. I have ups and downs like you can only imagine. Sometimes I do wonder if I have what it take to keep going, or if I can even be bothered.

But what are the options? Be a bum, just give up and do nothing with your life? Fuck that!

I have days of wondering if I have what it takes to keep going and to get to where I want to be. But after a few hours or days, I know I have to keep going. I know that until I can sit back knowing I have achieved all I was meant to do in my life, I won't give up. I'm not talking just money. I'm talking about contentment, happiness and love.

Life's a roller coaster and sometimes life hits a plateau and you just have to wait for the tide to turn and get on with it. So, if you feel like giving up, think about it. What you gonna do? ;)

One of the biggest things I have found that makes me want to carry on and to get on, other than wanting to be the best dad for my kids that I can be, is that I need to have something I'm truly passionate about. Something that I wake up in the morning and think about right away, something that positively consumes me. I have something like that at the moment in my life. It's frustrating because I can see what can be done with it, but I don't have all of the resources to make it happen yet. But I'll crack on and make it work.

So my advice to you is that you should never give up, no matter what. Find something in life that you are passionate about. If you are one of those people who wake up on a Monday morning dreading your job, then change what you do!

And if you ever feel like giving up (like I did in February this year), then just remember that life is meant to be lived. You don't have long, so live it on your own terms. So, what are you gonna do? :)

"Never give in!
Never, never, never, never –
in nothing great or small,
large or petty.
Never give in except to
convictions of honour
and good sense."

Winston Churchill

"We're born alone,
we live alone,
we die alone.
Only through our love
and friendship
can we create the
illusion for the moment
that we're not alone."

Orson Welles

Love

This is probably the hardest chapter I have had to write for this book, mainly because it confuses me so much, even at 38-years-old. There are different types of love that I have for different people; love of my boys, family and friends is a simple love. Not complex at all. The love for and from those people is easy to give and take and I think I generally am a deeply, loving person to those people.

It's the other kind of love that's a real fucker to work out for me. The love you feel for a partner. Being 'in love with someone'.

I think I have been properly in love three times in my life. Lisa and Kate were definitely two loves of my life. While with the third woman who shall remain unnamed, I'm still not sure if it was love. It didn't last long enough to know for sure but it sure felt like love and sometimes it still does now. Fuck knows, all I know is I am ready to love again. As I have said previously, the third woman certainly made me realise I could love another woman after Kate and in that respect, she did me a massive favour. Kate and I are still friends now, probably the best we have and ever can be. I like it that way; after all, we have two boys to bring up together still.

I say I am ready to love again, but part of me is scared still, I guess. I lowered my barriers to the last woman and all that did was to get me hurt. After seven years of pretty much being single, I can't help feel my life would be enhanced by having a loving relationship with a partner who not only is my lover, but my best friend too.

It's difficult though, because the type of life I lead and the work I do is not that conducive to meeting women and I am not the type of guy to just date as many women as will go out with me on nights out. I have to really like someone. If I get know a woman, I can grow fond of them if we get on. In many ways, it's the other way round. Once women get to know me, they know I'm a decent, caring, loving guy and not perhaps what they may have thought of me when they first meet me.

Timing is everything

It will be seven years in July since I became single. Apart from a few brief liaisons with women who were either passing people in my life, it has been single times for me.

I have never been the kind of guy just to hook up with anyone for the hell of it. Although there have been one or two brief encounters in the past, I'm someone who likes who I like.

I guess I have a type; there isn't much you can do to stop being attracted to certain types of people.

I have had many people tell me I should just get out there and 'have fun'. Translated, that means just go and sleep around for a bit until you find someone you may like to spend more time with.

The closest I got to this was when I came out of prison. For some reason, I attracted a few women, one whom I did have an 'arrangement' with, but I couldn't do it for long. There has to be depth and it has to be real.

Getting divorced and being dumped doesn't help with the confidence, I guess, but that's changed now. I see far too many nice women with total dickheads for boyfriends or husbands and I have changed my mind about myself (a little). Not saying I am the greatest catch to look at, I know I am a fat Matt Damon at best. On paper I'm not the best guy in the world to be with; my past has been 'interesting', to say the least. I wouldn't change it at all. Once a woman gets to know me, they like me because I'm not like many guys. I have had a few women (including my ex-wife) think that I was gay when they first met me. It's my feminine side coming out. :-)

Some things have changed in the last 18 months or so. I did meet one woman, who I did fall head over heels for. It wasn't planned, and I thought for the first time in over five years that I had met 'the one' but it didn't work out (for way too many reasons to go into here). If I'm honest, it finally made me turn a corner about all the regrets I had about not being with my ex-wife.

So I know at least I have the ability to love again. :)

The trouble is, weirdly, I'm not that bothered about looking for dates; because I have just figured it will just happen when it happens. I won't say it's not lonely at nights when I finish work, and Dave the dog doesn't talk back to me.

But I know this; I would rather be on my own, than with someone just for the hell of it. Life is too short to be with the wrong person in life. My princess will meet me when the time is right. Saying that, if Lyndsy Fonseca or Michelle Keegan are reading this and want to give me a ring, I'll probably take the call to arrange a date! ;)

Games

I have never been into playing games. There are women who like men to play games and to mess about. I guess I have never liked that, and I am certainly too old for games. Somehow I still manage to find myself in the middle of a game with some girls. A game I'm not willing to play.

To me, you either like someone or you don't. Like I have said, you can grow to like someone and that's great, but women and men for that matter who play games where people get hurt, well, that is not for me.

I have always valued partners and marriage and, in some ways, I think I was born into the wrong generation. It seems all too easy for people to give up on relationships nowadays. Saying that, if it's not working after giving it a good try, then people should move on.

As you hear from this, it's still a confusing old time for me. All I know is that I still hope to look over at my life partner when we are both in our seventies with as much love for them as I had, if not more, than when we met.

Looking to the future

I guess it's only a matter of time until I feel and find love again. Some poor unsuspecting woman will fall for me and I will fall for her back! If you're not into playing games, that's half the battle, I guess! :)

"I'm selfish, impatient and a little insecure. I make mistakes, I am out of control and at times hard to handle. But if you can't handle me at my worst, then you sure as hell don't deserve me at my best."

Marilyn Monroe

"Success is not final,
failure is not fatal:
it is the courage
to continue
that counts."

Winston Churchill

Success

What is success? Success can mean many different things to many different people.

For some, success is living a happy contented life, bringing up a family, helping others. For others, it's building an empire, a business that employs hundreds of people, owning things etc.

Whatever success means to you, you need to define it. I have changed my mind about success over the years and what it actually means to me.

Over the next few pages, I have put some ideas together that will hopefully help you to create a life of success in whatever way you want it to be.

"In order to succeed, your desire for success should be greater than your fear of failure."
Bill Cosby

Mindset

I struggle with mindset. Having the right mindset is something I have always strived to achieve. After everything that has happened in my life, maintaining the mindset needed to succeed personally and in business has been difficult for me.

No matter what your goals, your objectives, dreams or daily life is like, the biggest single thing you can master is to make sure your life is the success that you want it to be. It is about mastering your mindset. Something, if I am honest, I have struggled with many times in the past. No matter what though, it is always something I continuously work on and try to perfect. My ambition, tenacity, drive and sheer will to succeed are propelled by the long-term mindset I have developed.

If you want to make anything of your life, you have to have the right mindset. Let's say you have a job and you are working on setting up an online business in your spare time; you need to have the mindset to make sure you do what you have to do to get your online business going. Here is some news for you. It's hard to do. You may get home at night and family life needs to be seen too; time just flies.

If you are already working full-time on your online business, and working from home, you need to make sure that you manage your time correctly.

For instance, some people want to operate an online business for many different reasons, such as:

- Financial freedom
- Freedom from a nine-to-five job
- The ability to work from home
- The ability to work when and where you choose

When you are in business building mode, you need to keep reminding yourself what you are doing it for. This will greatly help to keep you in the right mindset.

Whatever your objectives, you still need the right mindset. I'm a workaholic and sometimes struggle with mindset from the non-work side of things.

Sometimes I work too hard; that is, I try to work as hard as I can but I don't work smart. It's a problem I've always faced. I will sit in front of my computer for 18 hours straight on some days, unless I take control. I have learned that you need little breaks from the computer in order for you to be as productive as possible.

If you struggle to keep motivated, set specific times for work and don't let ANYTHING stop you working during those times.

Rebel Entrepreneurs have a mindset that is different to other people. Focus, determination, not toeing the line and not doing what other people think you should do

80 / 20

When speaking on stage and during many of the webinars I have done on the subject of productivity, I have talked a great deal about 80 / 20.

Here are some of my observations my on 80 / 20 theories:

- There are two types of people: Talkers (80%) and Doers (20%). 80% of people talk about doing something. 20% think about it and actually get it done

- The 20% need the 80% in many ways

- The 80% need the 20% in so many ways

- The 20% need the 80% to sell things to

- The 80% keep buying from the 20%

- The 20% are happy with who they are

- Not all the 80% of people are happy and want to be in the 20% group

Can you move from being in the 80% to the 20%?

Sure you can - if you really want to.

WHICH ONE ARE YOU?

80% OR 20%

Even though I haven't got the exact life that I want, I am still in the 20% because I think differently to so many people. How do you think? How do you act? Which type are you now and which one do you want to be in a year from now?

Now I am not saying that all of us can be doers and in the 20% of everything we do. You can't be a doer and be 100% focused all the time. It's just not possible, no matter how hard you want it. It takes discipline to be in the 20%. One of the areas I really lack in being 20% in, is my health and fitness. Whilst I had time to focus on it, I got into the best health I had been in for years but since getting back into my business, it's a real struggle to maintain the weight and fitness I want. Partly because I work so hard, but partly because I haven't got the discipline to make sure I do the exercise. This will change now as I've committed to running a half marathon in September next year again so I have to get my backside into gear and get out there jogging.

So what I mean is being 20% doesn't naturally happen in all areas of our lives.

DECIDE WHAT TYPE OF PERSON YOU ARE....

"Success is going from failure to failure without loss of enthusiasm."

Winston Churchill

*"... if you don't have peace,
it isn't because someone
took it from you;
you gave it away.
You cannot always
control what happens to you,
but you can control
what happens in you."*

*John C. Maxwell
Be a People Person*

Personal Development

Like I said in the start of my book, I am frustrated and amazed that a high percentage of people in the developed world are not living anywhere near to their full potential and, in some cases, they just exist. I have never been one to want to be normal. Normal is boring. The thing is, why wouldn't anyone want to develop themselves personally? Ten years ago, the term 'personal development' was classed as a ridiculous thing, especially here in the UK. If you were into personal development, you were considered 'crappy'.

Well I disagree. Everyone should want to develop, grow and to become a better person.

My first real experience of anything personal development related was when I was given a Tony Robbins book. Then I went to 'Unleash the Power Within', a three day seminar he was holding in London in April 2004. It changed my life in a few ways. The whole experience changed my life, my mind and the future for me. I also thought I could help people like Tony does. One of my projects I will be doing soon is GetSuccess.com and this site will help people develop themselves and become the successes that they want in life.

If you could peek at my library, you would see hundreds of books, most of which are related to personal development in some way. I love the subject and it really 'juices' me to use a Tony Robbins term. And I love helping people with it too. I have helped everyone from my ex-wife to coaching clients and people in my mastermind group.

The feeling of having people credit you with helping them to change their lives is one of the best things ever and it is something that I will continue to do.

I urge you to start on the journey of personal development as soon as you can, if you haven't already. It's another world and there are tens of thousands of great people out there, ready to help you on the journey.

Entrepreneurs have it in their own interests to develop their own minds. Getting the edge in life and business is something that others can help you do; many of the best lessons in life I have learned from others have been via personal development programmes. You owe it to yourself.

"I'm a greater believer in luck, and I find the harder I work the more I have of it."

Thomas Jefferson

Luck

P eople say you create your own luck. Some people I know seem to be very lucky; things just seem to flow for them. I am not one of those people generally.

I think the harder you work, the luckier you get, but at the same time I think I have, in the past, pushed too much, tried too hard and pushed the limits which has affected my luck. It is possible that you can think work and try too hard sometimes and this definitely affects 'luck'.

I am a firm believer of the 'being in the right place at the right time' principle. But again you can help to create those situations by putting yourself out there and by making things happen. Some of my best ever 'lucky streaks' have been because I have found myself in the right place at the right time. Again though, I have created the situation for being in the right place to start with.

One of my best friends is the luckiest person I know; most things seem to work out for her. Others more similar to me seem to have the shittiest luck ever. I intend to change my luck and go to the bright side of the luck world. :)

I guess luck sometimes comes down to the amount of calculated risks you take in life and for me, I have taken some bad calculated risks in the past few years.

*"Sometimes when people
are under stress,
they hate to think,
and it's the time
when they most
need to think."*

William J. Clinton

Stress

As you have read so far, I have had my fair share of stress. Much of it some would say is self-inflicted. I think I have learned to deal with stress and my tolerance to it is probably considerably higher than most people. Saying that, stress and the root causes of it have contributed to my depression. Dealing with stress is something everyone has to do at different points in their lives, some more than others.

If you are an entrepreneur, you have to be prepared to deal with more stress than most.

Stress Relief

There a few things that can cause me stress including:

Time - Not having enough time is one of the main things in my life that brings stress. Yet, you need to take time out. Make time to de-stress and you will see big differences in the time when you are active.

Doing Too Many Things - I am the world's worst for taking on too many projects and therefore not having enough time. I try my best now to only have two things to focus on at any one time. (I like switching between projects that I am excited about.)

Health – Again, another physical and mental stress of mine. I get stressed or depressed and I comfort eat, which makes it even worse and when I am really stressed, I find it hard to exercise. But you have to push yourself. I have started walking in the evening too, which I find clears my head and gets me back in the zone. Getting back to good health and fitness is an important thing for me moving forward. You do feel better for it; it's just pushing the big heavy weight over the clifftop that's the hard part.

Relationship Problems – This is probably the biggest cause of stress for me in the past years. I don't have a relationship to get stressed about now. But the past sometimes does catch me up and stress sets in. If you are in a relationship and you have stress as a result of it, communication is the biggest single thing you can do to help. Talk to each other and try to sort it out and enjoy time together too.

Taking Time Out – I never used to do this, but I do now. I get twice at much work done after I have taken time out. I could never have written this book if I had not come away to France; way too many things would have got in the way. I try and take my weekends easier, especially when I am with the boys. Taking time out and not working 100% of the time is a big tip from me if you are a workaholic like me; it's hard, but you have to do it. Trust me.

Acceptance – I have never been great at just accepting things as they are. In the past, I have always looked back on things for way too long. Accepting the here and now of any situation is the best way of not getting stressed in the first place. I have started looking into Buddhism and acceptance is a big part of the Buddhist teachings. Learning to accept things as they are and saying, "Fuck it," to certain situations certainly helps.

Change – Change can sometimes breed stressful situations; one of the things I have learned many years ago is that change is inevitable. If you accept change, you will learn to not get stressed by it, it is something that will always keep happening.

Other things I do to de-stress is to listen to music. Music is a massive part of my life. I can turn some music on and my mood changes immediately; stress can go within minutes.

I love music; it's one of the most important parts of my life. Chilling with friends also helps too, sometimes I combine the two. There are a few others, you can imagine what they are; it involves women and a few Jamaican woodbines. ;)

Meditation

One thing I have found that helps me with my stresses in life is meditation. I do Transcendental Meditation twice a day. I started it in 2010 and almost every day I meditate for 20 minutes in the morning and evening. If you have never looked into meditation, I urge you to. The whole aim for Transcendental Meditation is that you are aiming for thoughtless consciousness i.e. being fully aware but having a clear mind. Over the three years I have done this,

I have achieved this many times and it's amazing. My friend Saj P told me about it and I thank him for it. It has really helped me. It's funny but after a good session, I either feel very tired and end up having a siesta or I feel totally energised and ready for anything anyone wants to throw at me!

To find out about Transcendental Meditation, just Google it. You will find centres providing courses everywhere in the world.

Stress can be controlled. It's hard but you can master being able to deal with anything the world throws at you.

Worry

Worry, of course, is tied to stress in a big way. I learned something a while ago. There is no point in worrying about anything. Of course, there will always be things you are anxious about in life. Ill health, concerns about your family and friends etc. But generally most of the worry that we develop in life is pointless. Worry does nothing positive; it just breeds stress and negativity.

Now I am the first to admit I have worried way too much in the past. It's something I am much better at now. One of the biggest things I did was to read two books that put a different perspective on worry for me, one by a friend of mine, Andy Shaw, called *A Bug Free Mind*, and the other, as I mentioned previously, called *F**k It* by John C Parkin.

Things always work out and something else I have learned is that sometimes situations just work out for themselves.

"Worry never robs tomorrow of its sorrow, it only saps today of its joy."

Leo Buscaglia

NOTE: If you want to help yourself out and read more about dealing with stress and worry, you should check out my friend Andy Shaw's book, *A Bug Free Mind*. It is seriously one of the best books I have read on the subject and Andy has a way of making you think differently very quickly. Well worth checking out.

I personally know, no matter what I say, I still worry and think too much. I never used to be like this; I think the year have taken their toll. Worry equals fear really. You only worry about something if you fear it in some way. You fear of the future, fear of making the same mistakes from the past. To fear something is negative in its self. Again, I am great at the theory of all of this, but sometimes struggle with practically doing it myself.

Thinking too much

This is something I am very guilty of. All my friends say I do it way too much. I know I do it too much. Overthinking things all the time clutters the brain with things that, in the end, don't matter in the long run. Now sometimes it is a good thing to think, but in other ways it's the worst thing to do. Instead of just letting things be as they are, I look into situations far more deeply than I need to. It's weird really as there is a part of me that acts very quickly on things, especially when it comes to business.

Thinking too much can come in the form of procrastination too; procrastination can cost you big time. Lost opportunities, lost money and lost chances in life.

It's a fine line between considering all of the options, thinking too much and worrying about thinking too much, rather than just doing and getting on with life.

Goals

I love setting goals. It's something I have always done. Maybe I have set too many in the past. But goals are something that keeps me focused and motivated. Setting goals in both my personal and business life is a must for me. A goal is just a dream with a date.

I urge you to set goals too. Personally I would set a realistic goal but perhaps on the high side of expectations and not quite hit it, rather than set goals that are easily achieved. But that's just me.

Here are some tips on setting your goals:

- **Conceivable.** That is, you must be able to articulate what it is about and describe it to your family and friends. The more vividly you can visualise your goal, the more committed you will be. For example, if your goal is to lose weight, can you visualise what you'd look like in that new suit or dress?

- **Achievable.** Do not set yourself unrealistic goals. Not only is it a waste of time, because they are unattainable, it is also damaging to your confidence and well-being. For example, what if you set yourself an unrealistic goal of making £100,000 overnight and were totally committed to it but then fail to reach your goal? How miserable would you feel?

- **Measurable.** You must be able to track your progress and definitively say whether you have attained a goal or not. Generally, the more worthwhile the goal, the more difficult it is and the more time it will take. Especially for these goals, it is important to have a yard stick to measure progress against. An example of a measurable goal is making £100,000 in six months.

- **Aligned.** Every goal you set for yourself must be consistent with your overall objectives, desires, expectations and beliefs. You cannot set yourself conflicting or contradictory goals. For example, making money online is not conducive to having as much free time (at least in the early days) as you might want.

- **Worthwhile.** Although not completely mandatory, I believe a goal should be challenging and worthwhile. Life is too short to be spent doing unimportant things. If you genuinely wish to improve your personal or professional life, set yourself worthwhile goals. Making more money is a worthwhile goal - it will improve the standard of life for you and your family

- **Desirable.** Not only is it important to have worthwhile goals, they must be goals you genuinely desire to attain. A desirable goal will command more commitment, dedication and perseverance from you. This desire will be your motivation. In our example, making money online is desirable because you can be more free to work when you want, make money whilst not working nine to five for someone else, you will lead a better quality of life and have more time for your kids, etc.

Rebel Entrepreneurs have goals, some pretty big goals. Your goals are your own, for your own reasons

Here is the check list for setting goals that I personally use.

My Top 10 Goals Check list:

1. My most important goals must be mine (There is no point in setting goals-based on what others are going. Do your own thing, be your own master of your destiny)

2. My goals must be meaningful (There is no point in setting goals and trying to achieve them if they are not of any real meaning to you.

3. My goals must be specific and measurable

4. My goals must be flexible

5. My goals must be challenging and exciting

6. My goals must be in alignment with my values

7. My goals must be well-balanced

8.   My goals must be realistic

9.   My goals must include contribution

10.   My goals need to be supported

S.M.A.R.T

You must set S.M.A.R.T goals. They need to be Specific, Measurable, Achievable, and Results Oriented and also have a Time Frame. You should spend at least an hour just brainstorming your own goals, write them all down and then prioritise them.

I hope this helps you to set your own goals.

Vision

You have to have your vision firmly fixed in your mind. What's your vision of your life? What's your business looking like in the future? What's your family life like? What's your free time spent doing? I made my life plan around four years ago. I update it every six months. I suggest you do the same. Just write down everything you want your life to be.

You have to have vision, do your own vision plan. Now!

The single thing ALL rebel entrepreneurs have is massive vision, a vision that is unwavering no matter what. They know exactly what they want to do, how they want to do it and exactly how they are going to achieve it.

Motivation

People get motivated in different ways.

One of the biggest areas of my life where I have had a love/hate thing is getting fit, losing weight and getting healthy. I have an unfortunate condition where I comfort eat if I'm down, stressed or depressed which doesn't help the waistline, nor does it help the motivation or confidence levels. It's a catch-22 thing.

I looked at myself in the mirror while in France writing this book. The weather was so terrible so I haven't done as much exercise as was planned, but I know one thing; no matter what, I am going to spend six months getting fit and healthy again. The mirror I looked in gave me all the motivation I needed! I've gone from Fat Matt Damon to Matt Damon wearing a bodysuit twice the size of him!

Seriously though, motivation is something very personal to everyone. People are motivated in many different ways; some by money, some by helping others, some by giving to charity, some by bringing up their family etc.

I know one thing about motivation I would like to share.

If you are doing something that deep down you don't want to do, you will have no motivation to do it.

No shit Sherlock, you may say to me, but hear me out. Many people find themselves trapped in a situation, in a relationship they don't really care about, in a job they just fell into. It's that Monday thing again.

If you truly are living your life as you want it, you will find the motivation to do whatever it is you have to do.

Believe it or not, this is something I have only just really learned over the last few years. Especially in business, I was the kind of guy that had all kinds of things going on, some of which I wasn't really that bothered about. I no longer do anything I am not motivated to do. Every now and then, we all have to do something we don't really want to do for whatever reason. That's fine, but 99% of the time, I am now only doing things I choose to do, and that's all the motivation to get things done that I need.

Think about an area of your life where you need to get more motivated in and then go about changing your approach today.

One of my things regarding fitness is that I feel guilty sometimes if I don't work out, so I catch myself saying I haven't got the time, but I know the more energetic I am, the more energy I will have, so an hour taken out to exercise each day would help in so many ways. It's the same with time out; I now try and have the weekend off. The motivation I have on Monday morning to get things done is amazing if I have taken time out.

There are many motivational book out there well worth reading, books by authors far more qualified to help you in this area than me, but I hope you can just think about what really motivates you and that it helps.

Fuck you, Motivation

Fuck you, Motivation. What's that? Fuck you, Motivation is one of the most powerful ways of motivating yourself that I know.

I have had many, many people doubt me in the past and still know people doubt that I will achieve things. Secretly some people like it that I have had my downs and are not too pleased about my ups. Well, this is FU Motivation.

Whatever you are striving for in life is personal to you. But when you have people doubting you and saying you should just give up or telling you that you shouldn't do something, well, it is just more FU Motivation to fuel the fire.

I have a group of people who I cannot wait to tell that I am sitting on the beach or living the life I really want. That's Fuck You, Motivation. Try saying it to yourself.

Success is the sweetest victory of all.

"*I was born with music inside me.*
Music was one of my parts.
Like my ribs, my kidneys,
my liver, my heart.
Like my blood.
It was a force already within me
when I arrived on the scene.
It was a necessity for me -
like food or water."

Ray Charles

Music

Music has been a massive part of my life; I don't know what I would do without music. I like all kinds of music, from Frank Sinatra to the Foo Fighters, Frank Turner and everything in between. Music motivates me, getting me in touch with my heart and the real me. It makes me happy and it makes me reflective. I'm listening to music the whole time I am writing this book.

Try listening to music when you are working and relaxing; it may help you too. I go to many concerts and for me there is something very special about experiencing a concert with a crowd of people who all love to hear the same music.

I have over 25,000 tracks in my iTunes catalogue and it is growing. Like I say, I really don't know what I would do without my music.

Music has the power to change your mood in a matter of seconds. I can listen to certain tracks and it is like a switch has been turned on in my head. For instance, someone pisses me off, and all I need to do is turn on a Guns N' Roses track and I'm back in the game. As part of my thinking, too much problem music helps me too. Some tracks I listen to help me to think better.

Music is a part of my normal working day. I always have the radio on or I'm playing iTunes. It's a motivator for me and you should have a think about if you can make it a motivator for you too.

Got some great tracks that in spire you?

Tell me about them here.

Time

When you were a kid, all the adults you knew used to tell you they can't believe how much you have grown up since they saw you last, and you as a child thought they were full of shit and just 'old'.

Well I'm that person now... and it makes me reflective. My eldest son has turned 13-years-old as I write this and I had a reflective moment last night. On each of my son's birthday, I have a cigar and a brandy as a cheers to them.

I remember the night I found out I was going to be a dad for the first time. A big cuban and a brandy were consumed and I reflected on how my life was going to change. Now I look back at the 13 years and realised just how bloody fast it has gone. It was weird. If I'm really honest, I started smiling at all the memories they, their mother Kate and I had shared. I played some Pink Floyd's *Wish You Were Here* on the stereo and had another swig of brandy. Then a few regrets crept up me and if I am honest, this has been the pattern of my life over the last few months. But then when I think about cuddling my two boys, I can only smile again. :-)

I haven't been the most sensible dad in the world ever, but one of the things that I have done, together with their mum Kate, is bring up two boys who have become great to be around and who are a credit to us both. At least I have managed to produce two great boys, eh?

Time flies. When I think back to the day Kate gave birth to James, I look back and smile. I look back at how our lives were and I look back with fondness. If you have read this far, you will know that it's been far from plain sailing. But one thing I do know is that life is for living. Who knows where I and my family will be in 13 years' time. I'll be 51 then, by the way, and I know I intend to live my life to the full.

It's true to say I have been running on less than half of my real self for the last six years or so, but I know with my boys as my driving force, I will be back where I want to be one day.

The older you get, the quicker the years go by.

As an entrepreneur, time is the biggest, most valuable asset you have. And it's the leveller for everyone. Everyone has the same amount of time in a day and week. It's up to you to get the shit done in that time. Rebel Entrepreneurs use their time the best they can, and in an ideal world you would work on your business eight to ten hours a day and be productive all during that time. Well, welcome to the real world. I have news for you; real productive time every day is no more than four hours a day, and that's if you're lucky. I have personally struggled with trying to be busy for the sake of it. Knowing in the back of my mind I need to hustle and be as busy as I can, but many times it just doesn't work.

Weekends have been something that have changed for me. I used to think I had to work seven days a week to 'make it count' and have a chance of getting what I want. I learned that having the weekends easier is a good thing for me, normally Monday mornings have a lot more energy behind them if I have had an easy weekend. I think for me the 80/20 rules applied to time too. I find that 20% of the time I spend 'working' produces 80% of results. And it's the other way round. I probably spend 80% of my time producing 20% of the results too. It's a struggle if you're an entrepreneur to be so focused and channelled about what you're doing that you can burn out pretty quickly. I have done it before and I'll probably do it again; it's connected to passion though. If you have the passion, you will do anything to get the results you want.

Treat your time as if it's the most precious thing you have. If you charge for your time per hour or per day, seriously consider what you could achieve if you were working on your own projects and business and charge accordingly.

This is the checklist I use as a way of keeping me on track and to help me to manage my time as best I can.

- Apply the Pareto Principle (The "80/20 Rule"). Work on the 20% of activities that produce the 80% of your results.
- Ask yourself, "Who can I team up with to get results? How can I build more effective teams? Who should be paired up on the team for best results?"
- Ask yourself, "Who, what, when, where, why, how?"
- Carry a small pad for tasks, notes and ideas.
- Catch the next train. Keep your trains leaving the station. When you miss one, don't hold your train back. Instead, catch the next one.

- Learn how to scan. Find and focus on what's important faster.
- Make minor decisions quickly. Don't spend $20 on a $5 problem.
- Improve your own effectiveness.
- Periodically evaluate how you are using your time.
- Remember Parkinson's Law – Work expands to fill the time available to completion. To waste less time, give yourself less time.
- Remember that time changes what's important.
- Use The Rule of Three to avoid getting overwhelmed. Limit yourself to three things, and think in three.
- Do it now vs. do it later. Avoid procrastinating.
- Don't let your inner critic or perfectionist get in the way of you taking action.
- Establish glide paths to simplify your day and make your routines friction free.
- Establish routines for recurring activities.
- Just start.
- Reduce the amount of procrastinating you do. Find your personal patterns for taking action.
- Start with something small.
- Take decisive action.
- Think in terms of "good enough for now", and treat perfection as a "journey", not a "destination".
- Worst things first. Do the worst thing in your day to get it out of the way and to avoid it looming over you.
- Add creative hours to your week.
- Add power hours to your week.
- Allow sufficient time for sleep and recreation.

- Carve out time for what's important.
- Have a buffer. You need a buffer to recover when things don't go as planned, or if plans change.
- Have a time and a place for things.
- Identify key windows of opportunity.
- Identify your peak performance times and guard them.
- Invest time each week in activities that free up more time.
- Know where your time is going.
- Know your most effective hours of work.
- Make appointments with yourself when to finish work.
- Say, "No," with skill to make time for priorities and to stay focused.
- Schedule time for administration.
- Schedule time for thinking and creativity.
- Schedule time for free time.
- Set a specific time each day for eating, sleeping and working out.
- Set boundaries. Set boundaries for your work week, such as "nights off", "weekends off", or "dinner on the table at 5:30".
- Spend time where it counts.
- Use your most creative hours for your most creative work.
- Use your most productive hours for your most productive work.
- Ask yourself, "What do you want to accomplish?"
- Identify three outcomes for the day.
- Identify three outcomes for the week.

- Identify three outcomes for the month.
- Identify three outcomes for the year.
- Identify what you want to accomplish each day.
- Identify what you want to accomplish each week.
- Map out what's important in your life to create a meaningful map.

Review your goals and objectives at regular intervals. Set reasonable goals.

> **Marky's Thoughts -**
> **Don't get old, live your life as if every day is your last, and say, "Fuck it," to stress and fear.**
> **If you don't, you will look back at your life and wonder where the time went. I for one don't intend to do that anymore.**
>
> **Live your life, love your life, love others, smile, don't regret and don't look back in anger.**
> **Time is the most valuable thing you have.**

Business

*"These are five things you'll find every successful
and passionate person has in common.
1. They have a dream. 2. They have a plan.
3. They have specific knowledge or training.
4. They're willing to work hard.
5. They don't take no for an answer."*
Nigel Risner

My first real business

I was 14-years-old when I started a first real
business. It happened without me realising really.

At 13, I had always been fascinated by animals; I
had kept everything as a kid. On a bike ride one day
whilst exploring, I saw a bunch of birds flying around and
saw that they were flying back to a shed. I noticed the guy
who was looking after them and, after a few days, went
up to him and asked him all about them. He told me they
were racing pigeons. These birds could fly hundreds of
miles and find their way home. I was hooked. I thought
that was amazing.

After many weeks spending time with Bob at his lofts, I
wanted my own. I persuaded my mum and dad to let me
get a loft and Bob gave me nine birds to start. Soon I
wanted more, so I joined the local pigeon racing club and

many a Friday night, I used to catch the bus up to the pigeon club to enter my birds in races. I wanted a bigger loft and one particular day after school, my mum said there was a loft for sale in the local newspaper. We went straight over to the guy who was advertising the loft and he said he wanted £250 for the loft or £300 for the loft with all the birds in it, and there were 60 birds. By this time, I knew a bit of pigeons and what made a good or bad one. I pulled my mum to one side and persuaded her I should get all the birds and sell all but 10 of the best ones. I knew I could make the money back, and pay my mum and dad back for the loft out of the proceeds. My mum agreed and that was it. The next week, I put an ad in a pigeon magazine and just one afternoon after publication, I had two guys arguing who was going to buy one bird from me for £60. So, I was in business. I was 14. Over the coming years, I learned as much as I could.

I went on to sell 50 of the birds for over £400. I was in profit, paid my mum back and had 10 of the best birds to myself. That started my career in pigeon trading. I went on to hold over 400 birds and buy and sell all around the world. The most I ever sold a pigeon for was to a guy in Japan for £6,000. I paid £2,000 for it and didn't need to pay for it upfront either; not bad when you are just 17-years-old.

Fast forward three years and I'm selling more birds in the UK than most. I was an agent for people and I took a commission. I went and did 'bird clearances' for people. It was a great business. By this time, I was renting some land from a local farmer to hold all my lofts which were filled with birds. December 2003 was a bad month though. On 6th December that year (I'm really good with dates by the way), I heard a knock at the door and it was the local farmer who told me my lofts had blown down with all of the harsh winds we had overnight. I went up there right away and was gutted at what I saw. It was devastation; out of 430+ birds, there were over 20 dead (crushed by falling wood), about 20 who had decided to stay around, but the rest had flown away. Now many of these birds didn't have a homing instinct because they had never flown out, but some of the most expensive ones were race winners that I was selling for other people; these birds had come first flying against thousands of birds. So, in theory, they knew this was home.

The weeks after this were a nightmare; this was my first experience of dealing with pissed off people. I didn't own half the birds I had, so I had some very mad men on the phone asking where their birds were. Over £38,000 worth of birds! I was fucked. Two particular birds had come down from Liverpool to be sold; they had come first and second in their races and were for sale at £450 each. After many irate calls from the guy who owned them, he insisted they hadn't flown home and wanted his money for them. This guy was a nasty piece of work. He somehow knew where I lived and that my mum was in on her own one particular day. He displayed very threatening behaviour. Needless to say, I had to borrow £900 to pay him back quickly. Still to this day, I am convinced he had those birds back but was just using the unfortunate situation I was in to take advantage.

That was my first big hit in business. I had to hustle for two years to pay the money back to people. My first big lesson in risk / reward.

It just so happened that I lived only a few miles away from the biggest pigeon breeders in the world. Before I started my pigeon business, I used to spend many a weekend up there looking at their birds. In 1992, the family purchased the world's most expensive pigeon, 'Invincible Spirit', for $132,000! For just one bird! This bird had won an international race against over 32,000 birds. This was a gold mine in my mind. Chicks from this bird sold for £5,000 each. This was a male bird that could be mated to tens of female birds every month. With each hen bird laying two eggs a time... You do the maths!

I was an agent for these birds, not a breeder. So I didn't see anything wrong with going to Louella Pigeon World, which the Masserella family owned, but others saw it differently. One Sunday morning, one of the brothers tapped me on the shoulder and asked if he could have a word. I was invited up to the big office and with most of the family present, it was suggested that maybe I shouldn't come down to the stud any more. That was my first experience of competition. It's true that I used to have vans full of guys coming down to me when they were planning to come to the stud and would buy from me as I was cheaper, but they had millions of pounds worth of birds and it was just little old me doing my agent thing.

During this time I wanted the world and more, especially when it came to pigeons. Pigeons were a living and not a bad one for the age I was, but I was not going to get rich from it. I guess I went against the grain a bit too much for some people in the pigeon sport and business. One particular person who did help me out was the editor of the biggest UK pigeon magazine at the time; David Glover helped me out of many scrapes throughout my career in the pigeon game for which I am grateful.

I decided I needed a change of direction. Being an agent was ok but hard work, especially after people didn't believe I would be unlucky enough to have my loft blow down (they thought I had just stolen them). Maybe all the rich pigeon races around the world would be the thing I could get into instead? The story continues.

> ***Marky's Lesson -***
> ***Learn about risk and reward quick and don't piss off the wrong people.***

157

"Mentoring
is a brain to pick,
an ear to listen,
and a push
in the right direction."

John Crosby

My First Mentor

I was young, ambitious and eager to get on so I put an ad in a magazine for a business deal I had in my mind. Sounds ridiculous now, but back in 1993 this is how things were done, or so I thought. Around the same time, as a result of putting the ad out there, I somehow became the potential mark in a Nigerian scam. This guy used to call me every day saying he had $38 million to invest. It still makes me laugh to think that I was about to fall for this, especially when you look at how common these scams are today.

Thankfully, it didn't take me long to find my first mentor, Harry Dann. During the course of my 'Nigerian investment deal' which lasted six months, part of my plan for my Nigerian investor friend was to find him real estate around the world he could invest in. One night I faxed over 100 real estate agents around the world who I found details of from within the International Real Estate Directory. My fax told them that I was an agent for a multimillionaire client who was interested in buying a property in their location. I'm still smiling even now when I write this as it sounds so bloody ridiculous. But I was a young, naive 17-year-old who wanted success very badly.

The next day I got a response back from one of the people I had faxed the day before. The phone call went something like this:

HARRY: Hi, this is Harry Dann from Freeport in The Bahamas. I got your fax yesterday.

MARK: Hi, Mr Dann. Thanks for getting back to me. Let me tell you about my client.

HARRY: Listen, is he from Nigeria? Yes? Well, I get one of these types of letters every week. Just ignore it and throw it in the bin.

MARK: No, this guy is for real. I have been putting this deal together for six months.

HARRY: I'm telling you, it's a scam....

And so it went on.

Eventually, I realised it was a scam. However, again, it was 1993 and I was very hungry for any sort of action. Thankfully, three days before I was due to fly to Lagos to tie up the deal, my parents physically took my passport from me. Remember, I was 17 at the time. It all seemed real. I have no idea what they were planning to do when I got there; I hadn't got a pot to piss in. At least one big mistake was sidestepped.

After talking to Harry a few times, I liked the sound of The Bahamas. Harry was an English guy, originally from Reading, who had moved there over 25 years before to get involved in the real estate industry. Over the coming months, I used to hassle Harry on the phone all the time, speaking to him a couple of times a week. I had something in my head. This guy was a business guy, I needed help in business.

My relationship with Harry grew. Eventually in April of 1993, Harry said during one of our calls that if I was that interested in The Bahamas, I better get myself over there and he would put me up and show me around. He had invited me down to The Bahamas to watch him work. I knew right away that this guy was all I had imagined and I was convinced that his mentoring would help to shape my business life. I stayed in The Bahamas for some long trips, hanging out with Harry in his office and seeing how he did business. I saw him and the property business and as I had just got interested in the Internet as a sales resource, I thought setting up a website selling real estate would be a good thing. I used to go to many big mansions in The Bahamas, whose owners were considering selling, and Harry used to take me along and introduce him as his 'Internet guy'. Back then, to have your property featured online was unique; I was his USP. We used to get into the car each morning and he used to say, "So, are you ready to start raiding a few corporations and to do some tycooning today?" Every time his secretary used to put me through to him, he always used to say the same thing. "Hello, my boy." This guy was a special man.

As with any good mentor, Harry helped me funnel my energy in the right places. "Go where the money is," was his advice. I was back in England and hungry for the Internet to make me money. I was working on some real estate sites but I wasn't getting any traction. So Harry told me I should go where the money is, and the only thing that was making any money online was adult sites. At first the idea just didn't appeal to me. I thought they were overly saturated and I didn't think I could carve something of worth there. But Harry encouraged me and I started in the adult Internet industry.

Over the course of the next six years, I used to visit Harry all the time and he saw my adult business grow. Many times after work, we used to eat in an English pub over there in Freeport and he would introduce me to his friends and people he knew. In many ways, he was not just my mentor, but my second father too.

Harry had many stories in his life; he had done many things. I set the plan up that I wanted to live in The Bahamas. Eventually I did that, but not while Harry was still around.

One of the saddest things in my life was when I got the news Harry had lung cancer. He was diagnosed around July 1999. I had just been over a few weeks before and had introduced him to Kate. We'd had a nice meal together one night, and he told me he had enough of the real estate business and asked if I could set him up with some adult sites. Of course, I said. But it never happened. A few weeks afterwards, I had a call with him and he told me the bad news.

I was due to go back over and see him in the October, but it never happened as he was in the USA getting treatment. Things were not looking good. Harry died on Millennium Eve around 11 a.m. All these years on and I still think about him all of the time, the amount of laughs we used to have together and the good that man brought into my life. It's weird. He was the reason I got into the adult business and a few years after he died, I eventually lived in The Bahamas and went on to screw it all up and lose all my money. I know if Harry had still been alive he would never allowed me to do what I did; he would have reigned me in. Funny old life, isn't it? I am fortunate to still be friends with Harry's son, Adam, who still lives in The Bahamas. He and I speak a great deal and I am planning a trip to go and see him soon.

I flew over to Harry's memorial ceremony on 9th January 2000. It was a touching day hearing so many people talk about my mate and mentor. I loved Harry and I will always remember him. Thank you, Mr Dann, you were a true legend, friend, second father and mentor to me and I owe you a great deal, my friend.

Mr Harry Dann - A truly special man

Harry once told me something everyone in business should remember:

"Business is a game, money just keeps the score."
Harry Dann

> **Marky's Thought -**
> **Always remember.... Go Where The Money Is!**

Your circle

The circle of people you keep in many ways determines the path in life you take. In business especially, I try to be friends with people who hold similar values to me. I have made the mistake of trying to 'get on' with people because I thought it would help my business. I have learned this doesn't work. You naturally work well with people you instinctively get on with.

For me, my life is split into two. Personal Circles and Business Circles. I don't have too many people within my inner circle on either sides of my life, but the people I do have are very loyal and special to me. I have been fucked over more times than I care to think about in business by people who, looking back now, were just with me for what they could get out of it.

I want you to think who you have in your own circles, in business and life generally. I actually write mine down and people move between different circles, depending on their actions. It sounds ridiculous, I know. I am a naturally trusting person but my circles list actually helps me to remember people I should be wary of based on the past. It also serves as a way of reminding me of the people who I should bend over backwards to help at any time.

Your network

I go to a lot of seminars. They have been responsible for a big part of my current success. You need to network in this business and seminars are a must. I'm going to three in the next month and it's not to learn from the speakers; I am a speaker myself now. I know most of the speakers worth knowing personally and can get any information from them I need in the bar. I go mainly to NETWORK. There is a lot to learn out of these events too. Many of the speakers you will hear are experts in their fields and you can learn from them. If you have never been to seminars, start going! They will help you meet people, learn and get on far quicker than just sitting at your computer.

In business, specifically your network of people is one of the most important things you can have. If you are good at what you do, much of your business can come from referrals within your network. Now I know professional networkers, these are people who just seem to go to one networking event to the other and never get any actual work or business done. I'm not suggesting you should become one of those people. Pick your networks and networking activities wisely. Ask yourself, in relation to networking events and organisations, "Is this network full of my kind of people who are right for me?" It's not just a take game either; it's about what you feel you can give to the group. There are many great networking groups out there for business. In particular here in the UK, 4Networking, which is run by Brad Burton, is a relaxed one that fuses the social side of life with networking and ultimately growing your business. But again, you have to do it right. Don't be a networking dick, who swans around being the big I AM!

> *Marky's Thought -*
> *Choose your friends wisely,*
> *choose your business associates even more*
> *wisely. Avoid the arseholes.*

Being Congruent

This is a term I only just started using in the last year or so. But it's a powerful idea. What does it mean? To me, it means being real. Being real with your thoughts, to people around you, and doing and feeling what you actually say.

For me, I have struggled with the 'Internet Marketing' (IM) industry for at least a year now. It didn't feel right. Pitching to people on stage who haven't got enough money, wanting them to buy a package that you believe in, but know most of them won't do enough work to make it work.

A big shift for me, perhaps to my detriment, is that I decided six months ago to be real, no matter what. I have put some pretty personal thoughts out online, things that previously I have never mentioned. I have written something called the http://realityreport.co.uk/ too. This report tells it how it is, in my opinion, regarding the Internet Marketing / Make money online industry. Something I have no real interest in doing anymore. Internet Marketing and all the tactics and knowledge is still very real and relevant but people want 'push button millions' and it's just not in me to give it to them, no matter how much money I could earn. I prefer to sell to real people, things that really work.

I urge you to think and feel what you REALLY feel, who you really are and act in a congruent way. For me it's been a release and a help. I'm not saying I went around lying before, I just did things perhaps that deep down I didn't want to do, but for whatever external influence or reason, I still did them. It's no way to live your life.

***Marky's Thought -
Be real, people will love you for it,
no matter what.***

---

*"Personal leadership
is the process of
keeping your vision
and values before you
and aligning your life
to be congruent with them."*

Stephen Covey

Jobs

What is a job? Normally a job means you go to work for someone else, get paid a certain amount of money for every hour or week that you work, you go home and do the same thing again the next day. If you are lucky enough, you will enjoy your job, but most people would rather do something else.

What a fucking waste of your short life!

I am not saying jobs are bad. Some people have no desire to be entrepreneurial and that's fine. But if you are wanting a job, at least have one you fucking like and don't mind getting up to go to on a Monday morning!

I only ever had one real job. I was 17 and I worked in a record store for three months. I hated every minute of it. I loved the music, but I didn't own the store so wasn't interested. My career in the record industry came to an abrupt end one Wednesday morning when a woman came in asking if we had any Barry White tapes. I said we hadn't got any as by this point I just couldn't be arsed to go and look. The manager saw me and we mutually agreed that I was probably better off doing something else. I haven't had a real job since.

Actually, I did have a job when I came out of prison, so for the first three months after my release I had that to do along with all my Internet Marketing activities but that was slightly different as I made my own hours and weeks up.

If you want to go it alone and get your business up and running, the problem is that you need to have a job to pay all the bills and support yourself and your family, but this cuts down your time to spend on your business. I have been lucky enough to start making enough money online within three months of getting out of jail - to be working full-time online makes all the difference.

Fourteen years ago when I started out online, I was doing my online business during the day (and not getting very far for the first 18 months) then driving a cab from 5 p.m. to 2 a.m. every night to pay my bills. My girlfriend at the time wasn't a fan of this but I kept going. Then when I found the thing that worked, I was working full-time online within two months. I realise the amount of pressure there is on the time you have. You have your job, your family, your spouse, all wanting time from you and I really do know how difficult it is. Depending on what kind of job you have and the financial situation you are in, if you want to do your own thing, I suggest finding a way of leaving your job as soon as you possibly can.

In an ideal world, you should find a way of saving enough money (or possibly borrowing it - I would myself, but realise this is not for everyone), and then take 12 months off your job! If you have a profession, maybe you can get back into it if need be. Try to find a way of leaving work as soon as possible. The ideal situation, once you have decided on your niche market and put the building blocks in place, is to find a way of getting your full-time job gone as soon as possible. Seriously, you will struggle to make a success of your online work if you have a full-time job.

Remember this... you will never be financially free and have the lifestyle you want if you work for anyone else... Just my opinion. ;)

It all depends, of course, on what kind of life you want... I know I would never be able to work for anyone ever again. I simply couldn't do it and I am probably unemployable.

> *Marky's Thought -*
> *If you are reading this and have no desire to be an entrepreneur, then that's fine.*
> *But just make sure you design your life how you want it and that includes having a job you WANT to go to on a Monday morning.*
> *If you want to do your own thing, save up as much money as you can and just go for it, leave wherever you are and get on with it, action is all that matters.*

*"Dreams do come true,
if we only wish hard enough.
You can have anything in life
if you will sacrifice
everything else for it."*

James M. Barrie

Sacrifice

I f you are reading this and already a serious entrepreneur or business person, you can skip this chapter because you already know all the sacrifice involved in doing your own thing. If you are unsure, then read on.

Throughout the course of my life, I have sacrificed a lot. There are some things I regret and would change if I could turn back time (there is a song in there somewhere). For instance, I didn't spend anywhere near enough time with my two boys when they were young, I was always too busy 'working', and they even went on holiday with their mum without me. What a waste of memories and time together.

I have also sacrificed personal relationships, girls who were not prepared or who were unable to play second fiddle to my business. That I don't regret because it's not as I have ever hidden my driving ambition. All the partners I have been involved with should have known from the get-go what living with me was going to be like. I never stop thinking.

The reality is, if you want to become a success you have to sacrifice a great deal in the early years. It's important to remember even once you have made it (whatever made it means to you personally) that things will be all beaches, golf course and plain sailing, because they won't.

Some of the wealthiest, most successful people I know are still incredibly busy. Most of them love it that way. I personally can't see a time when I ever retire. I may only do three to four hours a day and then dick around the rest of the day, but what are you going to do sitting on your arse all day? Answer... get bored easily.

You potentially sacrifice friends, relationships, time missed with loved ones and a whole bunch more. Like I have already said, I regret not spending more time with my boys in the past, but to be honest that's about it. It's my drive and ambition that makes me who I am. When I have my boys now, things are different 90% of the time I am with them. Occasionally stuff needs to be done when I have them, but you know what's cool? They are old enough to be interested in what I am doing and want to help and to get involved. So really, I have sorted the only regret of sacrifice I have made.

My advice to you if you are just starting out is to be completely honest with everyone around you about what is going to be involved.

Marky's Thought -
If it was easy, everyone would be doing it.
You just have to keep going if it's the path
you are meant to be on.

Support

Everyone needs support when they are doing their own thing. The biggest support you are going to need is that from a partner. Your partner has to be fully supportive of everything you are doing. Not that it's an issue for me at the moment, but when I do find my next partner, she is going to have to be there for me. It's a two-way street, of course, and I would like to think I will find someone who has her own things going on that I can help and be supportive of her too.

Many a strong and successful guy have had a strong and supportive partner behind them.

You need other types of support around you too; good advisors and mentors and professionals who can help you along your way. But I still say the most important support is that of your partner, if it is relevant to you. There is nothing worse than coming home and then having to work even more with your partner hassling you as they don't have the same goals etc. as you.

Building a support network around you is one of the single most important things you can do no matter what ladder you are on in your career or business life. It's not always what you know, it's who you know, and this has been so true for me. I have already told you how much a mentor helped me get me focused and ultimately was responsible for helping me to go on the right path to make a success of my online business at the time. Everyone should have a mentor. No matter what level you are at. The most respected and well known entrepreneurs had advisors and mentors. You should have too.

There is no better way to work your way through ideas and challenges than to brainstorm it and talk it out with people who you respect and value opinions of.

> *Marky's Thought -*
> *The most successful people I know have a great support network around them.*

Gambling

I have always been a gambler. Any successful person needs to take a few gambles in their life. I guess I have taken more gambles than most. I have gambled away too much in Las Vegas on the blackjack tables and once played blackjack on the same table as Ben Affleck. Me, trying to be 'Johnny Big Bollocks' and matching the big film star, but his pot got my arse kicked for $10,000 in eight minutes flat.

Gambling in business is inevitable if you want to get on, but you have to take calculated risks. I have learned this to my great expense. Going up against companies with pockets far deeper than yours is not advisable. Gambling relationships are not great either.

I guess I like the thrill of the gamble, but I have had more gambles go wrong on me in the last few years than before. Growing weed in a warehouse was a gamble that didn't pay off. Many gambles = Mark 2 - World 10+

You've got to just keep trying and moving forward but in the future, my gambles are going to be more educated. More calculated risks thanks out and out gambling.

Brad Gosse has always said I go balls deep into things. Maybe he is right. But with more calculated risks than gambles, I know that my future personally and in business mean I need to keep risking time, energy and money to get my next successes under my belt. It's all part of the game, I guess.

"Everything's a gamble, love most of all."

Tess Gerritsen

The Dream

"You have to have a dream. After all, as my latest tattoo says, 'A man is not old until regrets take the place of dreams'." - Marky

What's the dream, then? What's your ultimate dream life?

This is an interesting question I ask a lot of people. I'm not talking about lottery winning type dreams. You are more likely to get struck by lightning than winning the lottery. No, I am talking about a realistic dream for you in five, ten, twenty, thirty years' time.

So many times I have been coaching clients and I ask the question, "Where do you want to be in five years' time?" and the conversation goes something like this:

Client - I want to have a big house.

Mark – Ok, what's a big house to you, a mansion worth £3 million pounds or a nice four bedroom place somewhere in the country? What else do you want?

Client - A nice car.

Mark - What kind of car? A nice family seven seater or an Aston Martin?

Client - Erm...

Mark - Forgetting material things for a moment, what do you want other areas of your life to be like?

Client - I'd like a nice girlfriend.

Mark - Nice in what way? Good looking, nice personality? What about what you do on a daily basis?

Client – I'd like to have a job that I actually like doing.

Mark – Ok, so what sort of job?

And so it goes on. What I am getting at here is that you need to define your goals and what the dream is going to be like. Part of the reason why I am not where I want to be in all areas of my life is that I have very specific goals. I know exactly what I want my life to be like in the future.

What are your dreams? Write them down; write down what your life is going to be like in one and five years' time. Just go for it; don't hold back, you can cross out the silly stuff later, just write down the vision. You have got to have the dream vision in your mind all of the time. Believe me, it's one of the things that has enabled me to carry on sometimes. ;)

My personal dream life in the next five years is to live in my own built house on a specific plot of land that I want to buy. I want to have two successful businesses, a great partner and live my days on my own terms, not really doing anything that I don't want to do. That will do for now. ;)

> **Marky's Thought -**
> **Plan out your dream. After all, a dream is only a goal without a timeline. ;)**

The moment - fuck me, I've made it!

Have you ever had that moment? You know, the one where you say, "Fuck me, I've made it!" It could be about anything. It could be that you passed your driving test, you achieved the promotion at work or pretty much anything you set a goal for.

Well, my big 'moment' was driving along the freeway in Ft. Lauderdale and as I was approaching the airport in the distance and the ocean views lay ahead of me, it hit me.

It's May 2001. I'm flying back to my house in The Bahamas to see my wife and child; I have just come from my apartment in Boca Raton. I'm 26, my company is bringing in over £150,000 a month and I'm in the middle of setting up a new business that's going to take the company earnings to seven figures a month.

I smiled to myself, tapped the dashboard of the car. "You have made it, Mark!" I said to myself, and smiled again.

I had first travelled to The Bahamas when I was 18 and since that first day, I knew I wanted to live there. It took me seven years to achieve it, but I was living my dream.

That was my big, "Fuck me, I've made it!" moment.

When was yours? When was the time you couldn't stop smiling and realised you had made it?

I intend to have another one of those moments very soon! ;)

"It's clearly a budget.
It's got a lot of numbers in it."

George W. Bush

Know Your Numbers

T o live this dream life, you need to know exactly what money is going to be needed to do it. As you may have gathered by now, my businesses are mainly online, so all my goals financially relate to that.

I'm big into membership sites and I personally think this is the best way of creating a substantial recurring income online. Much of my focus in the future is going to be in online membership sites so I'm going to use this as an example.

Let's say you're looking to leave your job and work full-time online. You need $5,000 a month to live and support your family and pay all your bills; $5,000 a month means you are free and full-time online.

Let's say you set up a membership site in your chosen niche' the monthly membership amount is $47 a month.

You intend to have an affiliate programme in place so you can leverage affiliates selling membership for you and you intend to pay your affiliate 50% of the $47 amount.

The numbers work like this:

Monthly Membership Fee	$47
Affiliate Payout	$23.50
Processor Fees @ 5%	$2.35
Total Net Per Membership	$21.15
Online Business Overheads (including hosting, auto responders etc.)	$350
Your living expenses	$5,000
TOTAL MONTHLY $ REQUIRED	$5,350
TOTAL MONTHLY MEMBERSHIPS NEEDED TO	253

So from this simple calculation, you need to have **253** members paying you **$47** per month. It's not that many people, is it?

Remember that the aim is to have these people paying you **EVERY** month so you don't have to keep finding 253 new people each and every month. You will look to create so much value that when you find a member, you keep them for many months to come.

So let's say you set up your membership site whilst you are still working full-time and you put your affiliate programme together; you would need to find 42 new members a month for six months to replace your full-time income. Now if you pick the right niche, that's very realistic.

Now let's say your goal was to earn $100,000 a year. This would mean that your online business would need to generate $274 a day, which is $11.41 an hour. **VERY** achievable within the right market!

There is another number that you need to know and that's your own personal numbers.

Here are my personal number calculations, on the following page:

My Magic Number	
£300,000	My Goal (What is the amount of money that you would like to make each and every year that you work from now on?)
£0	How much did you make in the last 3 months?
£0	Current reality (x4)
£300,000	Goal
£0	Current reality
£300,000	**YOUR MAGIC NUMBER**
£330,000	x10%
	+Current Reality
£330,000	**YOUR MAGIC NUMBER**
What My Time is Worth	
How much do you want to earn in the next 12 months?	£330,000
How many hours a day do you work?	8
How many days a week do you work?	5
How many productive hours a day do you work?	5
How many weeks per year do you work?	46
How many productive hours a week do you work?	25
Total hours available to you right now to produce desired income:	1150
What you must generate per hour	**£286.90**
My Minute Rate	**£4.78**

Now what are these numbers about, I hear you ask?

Well, here goes. These are the numbers that I want to personally earn per month, year, etc. This is me taking money out of my online business as my own earnings.

I want to earn £300,000 - approximately $450,000 a year personally. Hey, I have a lot of things to do!! :)

So based on wanting/needing to earn £300,000 a year, and assuming I was starting from scratch, which I'm not, I want to work eight hours a day (in an ideal world - at the moment, it's A LOT more than that) and I want to work five days a week (again, not happening at the moment, but will be one day) and I also want to work 46 weeks a year and take six weeks a year off. Now, if you have read Timothu Ferris's book *The 4-Hour Work Week*, you will know he talks about actual productive hours in which you are fully productive, and I reckon I have about five hours a day. (These are hours where you are directly earning money and not just checking forums and emails, etc.)

So, based on this, I have 25 productive hours a week, which is 1,150 hours a year. This means I have to earn £286.96 per hour (About $430 an hour). This is what my hourly rate should be.

As a side note, I now have people asking me to coach them and this is a problem, due to the calculation I have just shown you above. My time really needs to be charged at $500+ an hour. (I don't want too many time-for-money jobs) I will talk more about this later on in another chapter. So let's work this calculation out if you want to earn

$60,000 a year yourself. Based on the same amount of productive hours, weeks at work, etc., you would need to earn $52.17 an hou ... this is what you need to value your time at.

So if you find yourself doing work or jobs that are earning you less than $52 an hour, you need to STOP DOING IT or outsource those tasks to someone else.

It's so important that you know these numbers... your numbers!

This is all part of living your dream. Without knowing what you need to be earning, you will struggle.

So, to review what we have just said:

You need to know how much you want to earn in your online business a year.

You need to know how much you want to personally earn. And you need to know your daily / hourly time value.

DO YOUR OWN NUMBERS NOW!

Money While You Sleep

For me the most exciting part of having an online business is making money while I sleep. I haven't yet got back to the dizzy heights of making $4,000 overnight but it's great to have online businesses that are able to sell things while you are asleep. There is no better feeling than logging online in the morning to check your accounts and see that money has appeared in your account while you were sleeping.

Back in the day, our companies used to make around £3.50 a minute, day and night, 24/7. It was a great feeling. What made it even better is that 75% of the income was a recurring income, i.e. we knew on average our members would stay over a 12 month period and therefore knew roughly what to expect in recurring income the next day.

For me, recurring income is the only way to make long-term sustainable money online.

Obviously there are offline businesses that can make money while you sleep if they are big enough and have enough people working for you, but with an online business you can work from home and be in the same situation.

I have criteria for any new business I get involved with. It is:

- **The business must be online**

- **I must be able to operate that business from anywhere in the world.** When my boys are old enough not to care about seeing their dad as regularly as they do now, I want to go back to living half the year in the UK and half the year in a permanently sunny place. :)

- **The business must have the potential to have a recurring payment element to it over time**

Most online businesses can be run from anywhere in the world and I haven't yet found any online business that cannot have a recurring income element to it in some way. My advice to you is if you have an existing business, either offline or online, look at the criteria above and see if you can change your business to fit it. If you are starting up, make sure the business fits the life you want and try and get a recurring income stream to it as quickly as possible.

Multiple streams of income

If you have a business of any kind, it is vitality important that you should develop as many income streams as possible for the business.

Multiple streams of income can come in different forms. It could be multiple products around the same industry or multiple sales channels to sell those products.

If you have an online business, you should have multiple websites bringing you income and traffic flows. Word of warning though, and I am guilty of doing this. Don't try to do too many things at once. Build one product or website up and get that earning and growing, then move onto the next website for the next income stream.

Things in business change so quickly. One of my friends, Simon, has multiple online businesses and niches. Half of his income comes from Internet Marketing activities, but the other half comes from niche business sites so his income is always flexible. One month he could be selling a lot of garden seeds from his gardening site, the next month, he could be selling how-to information. You have to keep flexible.

One of the great things about having an online business is that it is relativity quick, cheap and easy to set up 'test' businesses. It takes nothing these days to set up a website using WordPress and throw some qualified traffic towards the site. Very quickly, you will know if you are on to a winner; in many cases, for less than £100 of traffic.

"If you want to be a Millionaire,

start with a billion dollars

and launch a new airline."

Richard Branson

$5 Millionaires

What is a $5 millionaire, I hear you ask? It's a term my mentor Harry used to use. It's someone who is a wannabe. I'm not talking about someone who is nicely faking it until they are making it. I'm talking about the arsehole type who acts as Johnny Big Bollocks but actually has nothing to back it up, either as a person or financially.

I see them all the time, especially in the Internet Marketing Industry, it's full of wannabes. People who are standing on stage talking about their million dollar launches, but the reality is the launch did well to give them 5% profit and they haven't got a pot to piss in.

I have always tried to be real and tell it how it is. If I'm struggling, I will tell people. If things are good, I won't shout it from the rooftops.

There is a saying I like. "Money shouts, wealth whispers."

It's true.

Although the adult industry was full of arseholes, you didn't know about the people who were really making and if you did, it was only because you were in their inner circle. They didn't feel the need to shout about it. Nobody was teaching people how to do stuff; they were just doing it and making money.

A new market I am getting into is Bitcoin. You can see it there; there are many people just getting on with it. A refreshing change from the bullshit market of Internet Marketing.

The wealthiest man I personally know from back in the day is a Dutch guy, who started off as a bouncer in the red light district of Amsterdam. First of all, I have never met a Dutch person who I didn't like and wasn't friendly. David is a gent. If you met this guy, you wouldn't know shit about his wealth, but he is one of the wealthiest people I know. Up until 2004, he was sitting on millions and only driving a Volvo. Money shouts, wealth whispers, folks.

There is nothing wrong with not having money; I'm just saying there is a problem with pretending to.

You used to see $5 millionaires in The Bahamas all the time. Harry used to come across them in his real estate business. I once saw Harry do a deal for a piece of oceanfront land over dinner. At the time, I was just amazed that my mate and mentor had made $100,000 in 20 minutes. But looking back now, the guy he sold the land to was the kind of wealthy guy I'm talking about. Apart from his wife, who was stunning, you wouldn't know he was wealthy; he was just normal, but he had just sold his mail order company for $30,000,000 which back then was like being worth $60,000,000 now. You wouldn't know he was worth so much; he just did a deal with Harry for $1,000,000 of land to build his house on. No fuss, no fucking about.

The world is full of $5 millionaires.

Talk Is Cheap - Money buys land. That sign was up on Harry's office. I like that saying.

> **Marky's Thought –**
> **It's all about being real. Be real and you will be ok.**
> **Avoid arsehole $5 millionaires. :)**

*"The longer the title,
the less important the job."*

George McGovern

Number Plates and Fancy Titles

I t's the same with people that have personalised number plates and fancy work titles. I have to admit, I have had one personal number plate in my time and I would have again, but that's not the thing though. The thing is the show-offs, and the show-offs with nothing else going on.

People are obsessed with job titles. Director of Domestic Services = cleaner.

You keep your fancy titles, mate. I'll live my life without a title, thanks.

I know people. I had one guy tell me I was on my arse last year and what did I have to offer a woman? Yes, in theory he had more money in the bank than me at the time. But this is a guy that drives a BMW and not even a really nice one (I'm a BMW fan, by the way, just not a simple basic one) and has a private number plate. He lives in a normal house and probably has a few quid. But here's the deal. He goes off to work at the same time early every morning and scurries back facing traffic jams and delays at night. He then screws about at the weekend and does it all again the next week. What kind of life is that? And you know what? It would be ok if he was happy, but he is not. He lives in fear that things could change at any time. I can't imagine having to ask permission to go on holiday. Fuck that!

At least I live my own life how I want; although it may not be the best sometimes, it's my life and on my own terms, ok, apart from being in prison! I can sit in a coffee shop in the sun when I want (not that we get much sun here in the UK) but I can do what I want. Fuck your number plates and fancy titles, I'll stick with living my life as I want and doing what I want on my own terms, being my own boss, thanks.

Pissing about

It's easy to find yourself pissing about, doing 'stuff' but not really doing anything of importance.

It's the path of least resistance. You find employees pissing around all the time. If you are your own boss, the worst thing that you can do is to piss about. Worse if you don't even realise you are pissing about.

There is a reason you are pissing about too. It probably means you don't really want to be doing something, and there is no point living your life doing something that you don't want to do. Like I have said before, we all have to do things that we don't want to do sometimes, but most of the time you should be living the life that you want to lead and doing things you want to do.

Don't confuse pissing around with having downtime. I'm not talking about that. I'm talking about in the context of work and business. If you employ people, I can guarantee they will be pissing around some of the time. It's up to you to monitor it and make sure shit gets done on time.

Like I have said before, I am no good at managing people. I either let them run rings around me or I'm too hard. Having a manager is my solution; he or she can monitor the people pissing around and I'll just deal with one or two people in a day.

If you find yourself pissing around too much, ask yourself why. If you find yourself doing it more than a few times then you need to change your approach to what you are doing or change what you are doing completely.

Arseholes

The word is full of arseholes and I have attracted my fair share of them in my time personally and certainly in business. It's a fact of life that if you are putting yourself out there to get on in life, you are going to meet arseholes.

Some people are simply full of shit.

I have met many arseholes in my 20 or so years. People who have no intention of doing what they say they are going to do. With me, I mean what I say. I have been known to change my mind and have had deals go wrong, of course, but I will always be the guy who calls first to tell you if something isn't going the way we thought.

I have a list of people who have ripped me off. This list was started back in 1998 with a guy I was selling counterfeit note detectors for. I was his best salesman making him thousands a month, and one day he had a problem with his mobile phone so I let him borrow mine (back then, mobile phones were amazingly expensive to run) and this shit ran up a £400 bill on my phone. Arsehole. Even bigger arsehole that he never paid me back.

I met my fair share of arseholes in the pigeon business too. I was ripped off by a lot of people, including one guy that I did a deal with as a third party and he told the guy in the middle he had paid me for the birds; I was 18. Another £500 I had to stump up (that wouldn't have happened now).

Some guy in Florida took $15,000 for SEO services for my adult sites; and I never saw a single visitor from it.

I thought offering £2,000 coaching would filter out the arseholes, but truth be told it just attracted a few who had a couple of grand on their credit cards at the time. I had one customer last year who I gave over 250 customers to on their own email list; the guy never ever sent one email out to the list and then had the cheek to ask me for his money back! Arsehole.

Another guy (let's call him Mr Mustin Avenue) signed up to my coaching programme but cancelled his spot on my two day workshop 14 hours before it was due to start. I then worked with him one-on-one for weeks. He even asked me if he could have £500 back because he needed the money for Christmas, which I gave to him and he said he would pay me back in the New Year. I woke up one morning to a Facebook comment saying he was going to kill me! Why? Because he hadn't got any money, had problems with his partner and blamed it all on me for how his life was. He had the police called on him. Arsehole.

Perhaps the biggest arsehole I have come across in the last few years was a well-known Internet Marketer. This guy had trademarked his name. What fucking arsehole trademarks their own name? So he doesn't try and come after me for damages, let's call him Chris Knob. I met Chris Knob in 2010 and he was helpful to me. I had some money available and told him I wanted to get into CPA marketing (Cost Per Action). I met him and told him how important this was to me and that it had to work. I paid him $25,000.

He came up and trained me for two days. Most of it I already knew, so he then went away and pissed about doing nothing for months. This 'guru' was an idiot. No matter what, he wasn't going to pay me back. I put a website up about him, he got his lawyers onto me, and proceeded to flood Google with positive websites and pages about how good he was just to bury my site, then petitioned Google to remove the pages and hit my hosting company to take the site down. Since then, he has come after me for using his name. He wanted £12,000 from me. I have come across many victims of Mr Knob, some sad cases where he has just taken money from people and never should have done. He simply doesn't give a fuck and in my personal opinion is a con man. $25,000 is a lot of money, and he puts pictures up of him driving his Aston Martin and living the life. Not out of real results though, just through taking money from people and doing fuck all for it. Arsehole.

Mr Knob is still high up on my list of people who have done me wrong. Karma is a bitch, Mr Knob.

So you meet a lot of arseholes in life and you just need to build up your arsehole filter and figure people out for what they really are as quickly as possible.

Like I say, there are people out there who think I am an arsehole for whatever reason, but the difference is, I hope that I will try and make them see what I am really like so they can change their mind about me.

My advice to you, in business and your personal life, is to take a step back, do some research and find out who you are dealing with and to check out their intentions.

By the way, I have some arsehole who has posted about my supposedly scamming someone on a website; you can Google it at the moment. Funnily enough, two days after, I had a 'reputation company' emailing me saying they can remove it for a fee. Arseholes. If you care to read the post on Google, you will see the original person never entered into a conversation with me. Another kind of arsehole scammer.

> *Marky's Thoughts -*
> *Avoid all arseholes as much as you can.*
> *They will only cause pain, upset and sometimes massive financial losses.*

Focus

Part of having the right mindset, which has allowed me to achieve the results I have over the last few years, was my ability to be able to focus. Being able to focus on your business is paramount. It's impossible to remain 100% focused all of the time but you need to learn to be able to focus on your business for specific times and to focus on just one thing at a time.

As I am writing this book, this is all that I'm doing. I have turned off all my instant messengers, Skype and my email. I have put my phone on silent. All I'm doing is writing this book. You need to do one thing at a time and work on it until it is done. This doesn't mean that you can't have a few things on the go at the same time; I personally like to have a few different things to do. I know once I have completed the next chapter of this book, I am going to spend half an hour on one of my new businesses I am working on, and then will come back to writing this book; that's fine. But focusing on one thing, no matter how small that may be, is important in getting things done.

To get on in your business or to get your life on track and to become successful, you need:

<u>PURE FOCUS!</u>

Information overload

The other big problem I found with achieving my goals was information overload.

How many times have you purchased eBooks, never read them and have then lost them on your system? I have done this countless times!

One of the things I now ensure is not to buy anything if I won't act upon it within 24 hours. If I think it looks good, I ask if I can work with it within a day - if not. I wait to buy it. (Half of the time, I don't end up buying it.) The trouble with this business is that information is everywhere. The latest systems, latest courses and new eBooks are launched every single day; the list is endless. This can seriously inhibit your ability to work.

I still have a big 'To Sort' file that will not get looked at for a while. It's a pure waste of money. Stop buying things, if that's what you do. I have now come to the conclusion that I know all I need to know and I need to start concentrating on putting my own products out there and making money. After I decided this, it changed many things for me. I started becoming more productive and more profitable.

I thrive on being organised and use various Mac software to be organised. Evernote is one of the things I use all of the time. It allows me to file away information and to retrieve it in an instant.

One thing I do all the time (I did it to plan this book) is to mind map. I find mind mapping so easy and beneficial. I use a program called NovaMind for all of my mind mapping.

STOP GETTING INFORMATION OVERLOAD. Get organised, get productive and get profitable.

15 things I do to stay focused:

1.   **Have a 'daily to-do 'list'.** You should set yourself a daily to-do list. But every day I pick things from those to-do lists and try to accomplish all the items on that list before I do anything else. If you need a to-do list, a program I would suggest you look at is called Wunderlist. It's free and it works on Mac, PC, iPhone and Android. It's what I use every day.

2.   **Set time slots for people and work.** Set specific times for you to have personal/family time and work time. Make sure your family are aware of the times that you have set. They will help you stick to them and will understand when you say you're not available.

3.   **Set up filters in your email.** If you spend a lot of your time communicating and planning in front of your computer, chances are you deal with emails on a frequent basis. Setting up filters in your email client can be a great way of sorting out what's important and urgent, from personal stuff which can wait. Instead of dealing with a single inbox with

hundreds of unread email, you only need to deal with smaller folders categorised by project, priority and context. I use www.gmail.com for my email. Every website I have has domain forwarding to gmail.com and I have labels set up for each of the different sites I run. I can't recommend gmail.com enough!

4. **Check email at certain times.** Set specific times to check emails. My friend Brad Gosse has taken Timothy Ferris's *The 4-Hour Work Week* practices and only checks his emails twice a week. With the amount of things I have going on and the amount of deals and people I'm working with, I simply can't do that. So I check my email first thing in the morning and in the evening only. I have also set up another private email address where certain important people, who I need to hear from instantly, can email me without delay. I use this email address and it creates a specific alert on my computer if one of these emails comes in. I suggest you set a specific time to check email only at those times and if need be set up a specific 'VIP email address'.

5. **Set your IM status.** If you use Instant Messenger or Skype when you don't want to be disturbed, make use of the status and set yourself as being away or busy. Your friends and colleagues will honour that. They can either send you an email or look you up later when you aren't as busy. I set my Skype status as 'Do Not Disturb', which stops all messages coming through to me until I set my status back to being available.

6. **Listen to the right types of music.** Music is a great way of settling into the working routine.

7. **Fill up a water bottle.** Keeping yourself hydrated is very important for all sorts of health reasons. Instead of going to the tap with your glass every hour, try filling a water bottle at the start of the day.

8. **Turn off your phone.** Just do it when you're working. If it's urgent, they will call back when you're free.

9. **Get a good chair.** If you sit for long hours at your desk, and I'm sure some of you do, you might find it helpful to get a good chair. I find it pretty hard to stay focused when my neck and back are sore because of a bad set up at my desk. A good chair can eliminate much of this, allowing you to work for long stretches without breaks and physical distractions.

10. **Use shortcuts on your computer.** If you find you do the same thing with your computer more than once throughout the day, you might find it helpful to look for ways in which you can do them without too much manual repetition. For example, if there's a project folder you access all the time, try adding a shortcut to your Explorer or Finder so you can get access to it with a single click, instead of expanding folder after folder in the tree panel.

11. **Close programs you're not using.** As an Internet Marketer, I use a lot of programs important to my work. However, in most cases, I only need a few applications open at the same time. Instead of Alt-Tabbing constantly and fighting the computer to locate the program you need, try only having the applications open that you need. Close everything else. For example, if you have already located a file and no longer need a particular Explorer or Finder instance open, close it. There's no reason at all to leave it around.

12. **Limit time on Facebook, Twitter, news sites and blogs.** I don't think I need to say too much about this. Facebook, Twitter, Tumblr, news and blogs can be great from an interest perspective, but they really can take you away from the project you should be working on. Try to limit going to these sites during your working time.

13. **Change your mindset and make work fun.** For me, I find it difficult to stay focused on doing things I'm not naturally interested in doing. In most cases, there's probably nothing I can do about it. However, be mindful of the fact that your perception of work is something you can control. For my last tip here, I suggest you try changing your mindset or turning work into a game. An unfocused mind is an unchallenged mind. So make things fun!

14. **Having well-defined goals.** I can't stress the importance of this enough. Having goals which are well-defined is the key. Write them down. Whenever I get distracted, I read my goals and I'm reminded of what I am trying to do and why.

15. **Breaking things into bite-sized chunks.** Having broad, high-level goals are good but having an actionable plan is essential. A plan can identify how you can get from where you are to where you want go. Breaking goals into smaller actionable chunks (tasks) is great – it gives me motivation to start and allows me to get things done in one sitting.

I would like to give a warning here. It's one thing to be organised and know exactly what you have got to do on Monday morning or for the week ahead but totally another to actually getting the fucker done!

This is something I am bad at doing, totally bad, especially during bouts of depression. Even without depressive bouts, I can be bad at it. I try now to only focus on two things in any one day. It works better for me, but I still kick myself at the end of the week and ask myself what I have achieved some weeks. Being an entrepreneur involves getting shit done, and getting things done that earn money, bring in leads and bring in cash. No difficult when you say it like that, but you know what? Life gets in the way of this idealism. All you can do, like I do, is try and stay organised and focused as much as possible. There are some great systems out there for organising your self.

I personally follow the GTD system (Getting Things Done) or try, at least! ;)

> ***Marky's Thought -***
> ***The ability to focus is the single most important thing you can learn in your life and business.***

The Real You

Who is the real you? This is a question I have often asked myself in the past few years. Asking myself if striving to build my entrepreneurial empire was really what I wanted (the answer is still yes), but also deeper than that. Who I am really and the person I really want to be. The answers that came back were not necessarily ones that I wanted.

I fell into the trap of becoming someone doing something I didn't want to do. I thought I wanted to be the next Internet Marketing guru. It turns out I didn't. I didn't learn that until I had done speaking gigs in front of 300 people, which at one point was one of my goals. It just didn't feel right. I love speaking but not having to sell at the end. Funny thing though. The real me is the me when I am on stage and speaking; it's just the selling bit I found hard. I found it hard because I worried that the people I was talking to were not right for the product I was selling. The product I was selling was great, but my heart just wasn't into my audience before me. Don't get me wrong, I loved the audience, but it just didn't feel congruent to sell my product to 90% of the people there. You may wonder why, but deep down I knew 9% wouldn't do anything with it.

So that is one example of me not being the real me.

The real me is a happy-go-lucky, friendly and smiling guy, wanting to help people and not being stressed at all.

I have done way too many things in my life that I didn't really want to do and I just did them for one reason or another. Either I needed the money or I was just doing it to help people out who I really shouldn't have felt that I needed to help out.

Living your passion

For me, it's all about living your passion. What juices you? What excites you daily? That is one of the big things you have to ask yourself. If you can crack the answer to this, then you are halfway to finding your real self.

Ask yourself what your passion is? Don't know right away? Spend some time thinking about it. Spend some time asking what you would like to do every day.

What would you do if money wasn't an object?

Another great way of finding the real you and, more importantly, finding your passion, means asking yourself what would you do daily, weekly and monthly if money were no object? You may say that this is bullshit because money is an object. But you may surprise yourself. Many people could live their lives as if money were no object with a structured plan over a few years. Things can be achieved.

What people think about you

There are always going to be people who you care about. These are the people who you care deeply as to what they think about you. But they, for me anyway, are few and far between. Most other people, I just don't care.

If you can adopt this attitude, it will help you to be the real you and help you to live that real life even more. After all, whose life is it?

Owning your life

Tell me, what is the point in living anything but your own life? There is none. The average life expectancy in the UK is 85 years for a man and 89 for a woman. That's 1,020 months, 4,420 months and only 31,025 days, and that's if you are lucky enough to live to 85-years-old. Not a lot really when you think the world is 14,500,000,000 years old. We are a mere blip in the world as it goes by. Living anything other than your own life is just waste. Think about it. Do you want to waste it or to live it on your own terms?

The bigger picture / making a difference

For me, the big test will be looking back at my life when I am near to dying. If I am lucky enough to be compos mentis 24 hours before my eventual death, I would like to look back and think I lived it my way, and what a fucking life it was. I'd also like to make a difference and be someone people still talked about years after their death. I have mentioned people like my first mentor Harry and Sir Freddie Laker; both of those guys made a difference in the world. They will be remembered and talked about by many people in the world years after their death. Obviously there are many, many people like this; people who will always be remembered in their own way. But the sad fact, however harsh it may sound, is that there are many people that won't be remembered.

I have no intention of being someone that is forgotten easily. Do you want to be?

"Follow your passion, follow your heart. They will lead you to the place you want to go."

Evelyn Glennie

Being An Entrepreneur

I f you are reading this, then the chances are that you are either an entrepreneur already or wanting to start the journey. Although I would not change being an entrepreneur for anything, I have to warn you, it's not as easy as some people would make out. It's hard, it demands far more of you and your time than if you had a regular job. But the rewards over time far outweigh sacrifices in my opinion.

Do you have what it takes?

Do you have what it really takes to be successful as an entrepreneur? Long days, even longer nights, partners not being happy with you and people trying to screw you over all the time.

It's hard. It's hard to build up the resilience that is needed sometimes. And you know what? Honestly, I don't have as much resilience as I used to have 15 years ago! I find it harder to keep going sometimes. I'm not sure if it's an age thing or just the amount of bullshit and tests I have had in the last years. I suspect it's to do with the level of stresses I have had.

Have I put you off yet? No? Great.

Like I have already said, I would not change my entrepreneurial life and I can't imagine ever being anything different. I reckon I am unemployable anyway. The long road of being an entrepreneur and the success you get eventually after working your arse off is worth all of the effort. Make it fun on the way and you are winning already.

What are you doing it for?

For me, my aims and goals haven't really changed much in the last 14 years – but how I intend to achieve them has changed. For me, I still want to be financially independent and I still want to be able to choose how I spend my days, weeks and years.

The difference now is that instead of just having one goal of making millions of dollars from nothing, like I did 10 years ago, I now have measurable stages to my goals.

My goals are split into a five stage plan. Each stage has specific financial and lifestyle aims. I had the weird experience of sitting in my prison cell watching Frank Kern's *Mass Control* programme in April 2009. In one of the videos in this course, Frank talks about a time in his life where he had "made it"; he had every conceivable "thing" you could want, great house, cars and family living in Georgia.

This video was very powerful because in it Frank says he realised during this time that he wasn't happy with any part of his life. He moved across the country, completely closed down most parts of his business that he was unhappy with and started all over again in California.

If you get a chance to see this video, please make sure you do. It is very powerful.

The reason I mention this is twofold. Firstly, I was sitting in a prison cell listening to Frank Kern talk about how completely terrible it was that he has all these "nice" things and how his life sucked. I'm sitting there £250,000 in debt, not able to get out of prison and see the outside world for months. I thought, "What do I really want?"

After a few days of hard thinking, I decided to proceed to write my life plan, which is over 100 pages long.

For me, my 'end game' result hasn't changed much from 14 years ago. I want a net worth of over £15,000,000 and to have a life living half of the year in the UK and half in a sunny climate. But the process of visualising exactly what I want has helped me today to keep focused and to maintain my work ethic. It also makes sure that I don't stray from the end game result. The other big difference is how I will get there. I have these five stages to my end game plan, which is a great deal better than before.

The second reason I mention Frank Kern is that it got me thinking exactly how many people wonder what they want. Many people think they know what they want, but they haven't really visualised what it would be like.

Many people think they want "lots of money" and "to work for themselves", but they haven't measured it. Exactly how much money do you want? What are you going to be doing when you have your own business?

I don't want to go into this subject too much more in this report as this is about how I made $5,000 a month. But do ask yourself what you really want as your answer could be surprising - maybe what you thought you wanted isn't actually what you really want at all.

I intend to do another eBook about mindset and personal development, in which I will talk more about this subject.

But in the meantime, just ask yourself what you really want from life? You don't want to end up like Frank Kern, earning millions of dollars a year, but living a completely unhappy life.

There are the five things you'll find every successful and passionate person has in common:

- They have a dream

- They have a plan

- They have a specific knowledge or training

- They're willing to work hard

- They don't take no for an answer

Life fundamentals

- Know what you want

- Know why you want it

- Discover your talents

- Use your talents daily

- Work hard

- Work smart

- Give unconditionally

- Love unconditionally

- Find your purpose

- Live your purpose

"Hell, there are no rules here -

We're trying to

accomplish something."

Thomas A. Edison

Breaking Rules

For me, some rules are there to be broken. Whose rules are they, anyway? Normally, someone is putting them in place and they are designed to keep you down.

Being an entrepreneur, it is much easier to ask for forgiveness after the fact than seek permission before you do something.

You will always have the situation where others' perception of right and wrong is different so some people think that breaking rules is wrong and should never be done. I disagree. I think some rules are ridiculous, especially in business.

A fine line

There is a fine line, however. Yes, I know I have broken rules in the past, and yes, I have broken laws in the past, which was stupid, looking back. I'm not suggesting for one moment that people should go out and break the law. That's just not advisable.

I will, however, say there are two ways of looking at my past. I like to think I would never do anything to hurt anyone. The laws I broke were for growing a plant (or a few hundred). One observation I made is that there is a fine line between being an entrepreneur who pushes the line a bit too much and of being a criminal.

In fact, it hit me in prison that some of the guys I was locked up with are some of the best entrepreneurs in the UK. If they channelled their skills and knowledge into legal activities, they would become huge successes. Problem is, for most of them it just takes longer to achieve than illegal activities.

(NOTE: I would be lying if I said I hadn't thought about doing something else that crossed the line after I had come out of prison, but I also know this; I would never want to go back to prison ever, horrible places. I couldn't do it to my family and I promised my mum I wouldn't ever do anything knowingly that could put me back in there. You know what? My luck with that stuff wasn't the best, was it really? :)

I'm sticking to the right path, the harder one, but the one that will work out and get me exactly where I want to be, with hard work, dedication and time and with a bit of luck.

If people don't know me, they might think that I'm an ex-porn peddling, drug dealing, scumbag. Where as I would like to think I just pushed the entrepreneurial line too far and went where the money was (well, when it came to porn, anyway) and did a stupid thing out of desperation i.e. the pot.

> ### *Marky's Thought -*
> *Watch that fine line, don't step over it and if you catch yourself being tempted to go to the dark side, think again. Look what happened to me.*

Working Too Hard

I am the world's worst for working too hard. Working too hard and not being smart enough is a big problem for me. Working for too many hours and feeling guilty when I am not working has been a problem for me too. I think I have changed a lot in the last few years but I still ask myself if I am working hard enough.

I think the problem is that you have more energy when you are younger. I know that sounds a bit crap but I think it's true.

For me, taking time out makes me work much better and more effectively when I come back to work. That being said, if work needs mean meeting deadlines, then it gets done. That's the flexibility you have when you are an entrepreneur.

I think I get my work ethic from my dad and the idea if you are not working, then you are not doing well enough. My best friend, John, is the same. Don't get me wrong, I am instilling a strong work ethic into my two boys. I want them to realise they have to work hard to get to where they want to be and to not just have an expectation that the world owes you a living. That entitlement mentality bugs the crap out of me.

> *Marky's Thought -*
> *Don't work too hard that you burn yourself out.*
> *Work smart and not hard. Trust me, it is better.*

"There are risks and costs to action. But they are far less than the long range risks of comfortable inaction."

John F. Kennedy

Taking Action

You have to take action.

You hear everyone saying it time and time again, but you have to. Without action, those first steps to starting something you go on a road to nowhere.

This is what I did to take action and to start earning within two weeks of getting out of prison.

- I started posting on the WarriorForum (an internet marketing forum)

- I decided with Brad what product I could create that wouldn't cost me anything but my time

- I created that product

- I launched it as a WSO (Warrior Special Offer) for $7 and kept increasing the price. I was making a profit within three hours of launching the product. Time taken = four hours. Profit to date = $2,000 +

- I thought of another product, created it, launched it as a WSO. Time taken = five hours. Profit to date = $1000 +

- I took an eBook that I had created in prison - edited it with up-to-date information, launched it on the WarriorForum as a WSO. Time taken = three hours. Profit to date = $500 +

- I got all my notes from Russell Brunson's workshop, typed them out, made an audio and video walk-through of those notes and launched that. Time taken = eight hours. Profit to date = $1000 +

- I did my first free WSO as a list builder. I gave away a 30 minute recording of Brad and I. Time taken = two hours. Subscribers to date = 500 +

- I launched 'My Millionaire Mentor Coaching' calls, offering membership to all of the coaching calls we have done so far. Offered at $2 on a three day trial. Hundreds of members to date

- Then I started concentrating on non WarriorForum activities. I just created products and promoted them on the WarriorForum and through Facebook, Twitter etc.

- It's all about ACTION guys, that is all you need to do. Decide you are going to do it and DO IT.

Listen... I have problems all of the time, things come up, days go wrong and things don't go to plan. I get very frustrated. But you just have to keep going. Massive Action = Massive Result.

But you have to stick with it. Keep going and never give up. If I had given up, my parents would have lost their house and I would have been living in a cardboard box somewhere. With all the negative things that have happened to me in the last 10 years there were one or two times (for a short while) that I thought, "Fuck it! I've had enough," ... but those thoughts lasted no more than a few minutes. You are either a talker or a doer and I'm a doer. Are you?

If possible, you need a good support structure around you too. Get help from friends and family in your quest to achieve whatever it is that you have set as your goals. If you have negative people around you, distance yourself, quick. Negative people suck all your energy and will not help you in anyway.

And don't listen to the people saying you can't do whatever it is that you want to do.

Fuck them ;)

Just get on with it and get it done... but... like I say, YOU have to **TAKE ACTION**.

Write an action plan of what you are going to do and get to it.

By the way... if you can find a mentor, do it. A coach/ mentor is one of the best things anyone can do to help them succeed as they push you to action, just like Brad did for me and I have gone on to do for many people since. It's a great way of making you accountable for your own actions. One single call from your mentor or coach can give you everything you need to take action immediately.

FIND A MENTOR OR COACH!

Importantly.....

TAKE BLOODY ACTION!

NOW

RIGHT NOW

GET TO IT

CHANGE YOUR LIFE

STOP THINKING ABOUT IT

DO IT!!

You will thank yourself and it will happen sooner than you think.

Money

Harry taught me that money is just a tool. A tool to get you doing things more quickly than if you haven't got any. Money is freedom too. I was once way too caught up on just the money. If you focus just on the financials, you will lose out. Money is only a tool in the entrepreneurial tool box to make things happen.

The freedom part is the fun part, both personally and in business. The freedom to do new things and to explore new opportunities comes with money. Personally you can have a great time with money too.

It's all about the experience, folks.

> **_Marky's Thought -_**
> **_Treat money with respect and it will see you right._**

"Productivity is never an accident.
It is always the result of a
commitment to excellence,
intelligent planning,
and focused effort."

Paul J. Meyer

Making It Work

I f you are already an entrepreneur or are starting on the journey, there are many things you need help with and many things you can do to make sure things work for you.

I talk about a few of those things in the coming pages.

(I have plans to publish other books specifically on topics about working as an Entrepreneur. If you want more information, check out the link to my other books at the end of this one.)

Productivity

This is a short blast of some basic information about productivity and systems. There are many great books written entirely on these subjects and this book was never intended to be one of those. Here are a few observations from me on products and systems you can put in place to make your business work better.

Productivity is one of the biggest challenges you have if working on your own thing. It's real easy to get distracted, especially when you have an online business. After all, distraction is just a click away.

Here are my top eight tips to be productive when working online:

1. Working where you live, sleep or should relax is counterproductive. Separate your environments – designate a single space for work and solely work – or you will never be able to escape it.

2. Perform a thorough 80/20 analysis every two to four weeks for your business and personal life.

3. Striving for endless perfection rather than accepting great or simply good enough, whether in your personal or professional life, is pointless. Recognise that this is often just another "Work for Work Sake" (W4W) excuse. Most endeavours is just like learning to speak a foreign language; to be correct 95% of the time require six months of concentrated effort, whereas to be correct 98% of the time requires 20 to 30 years.

4. Blowing minute problems out of proportion as an excuse to work is pointless.

5. Making non-time sensitive issues urgent to justify work is counterproductive.

6. Viewing one product, job or project as the be all and end all of your existence is wrong. Life is too short to waste, but it is also too long to be a pessimist or nihilist.

7. Ignoring the social rewards of life. Surround yourself with smiling, positive people who have

absolutely nothing to do with work. Create your muses alone if you must, but do not live your life alone. Happiness shared in the form of friendships and love is happiness multiplied.

8.   Answering email that will not result in a sale or that can be answered by a FAQ or auto responder must not be done.

I could write pages and pages on this subject but I won't. Find some great book suggestions on this topic at the end of this book.

Systems

I have never been great at developing systems; I have always been the guy that just wants to get on with things. But the reality is, if you are going to grow your business, you need to have systems in place. Now I have other people to duplicate the tasks and systemise them along the way. This way we can give that same task to other people who are new to the business time and time again. Rinse and repeat.

This all ties into expanding your business and outsourcing tasks over time. If you have systems in place to run every part of your business then that business, in theory, can run without you, grow and keep making money, even if you are on holiday.

There is a fine line with building systems. Over complicating the process can have a counter effect on people's productivity.

There is not one task in an online business that cannot be systemised and few tasks that cannot then go on to be outsourced.

Combining productivity, systems and a great to-do list into your daily routine can mean the difference between working hard and working smart. Working smart is something I have struggled with in the past. But the reality is that 80% of my income and business comes from the 20% of the time I'm working hard.

It's that 80/20 rule again.

Finding Your Flow

I f you have ever lost all track of time and have been so absorbed in your work, then you will have experienced 'Flow'.

There is no better feeling than being in the flow and getting things done. Flow makes you feel good, increases productivity, time flies and you feel like you have achieved much at the end of your flow session.

You get fully immersed in the positive mental attitude that is created by flow.

You forget about you, about others and everything around you, you are completely focused on the task at hand and you lose all track of time whilst feeling happy and in control.

The result is you become more creative and more productive.

Sometimes all of life seems to flow and things just click into gear and all come together at once.

Some tips on achieving flow:

1.   Choose work you love - and flow will be halfway achievcd alrcady.

2.   Choose important tasks. Make sure you pick the most important tasks.

3.   Get Challenged. Challenge yourself; don't pick the easiest tasks.

4.   Find your peak time. We all have a peak time to work. Mine is around four to seven p.m. after my siesta.

5.   Get rid of distractions. Turn everything off and only focus on the one thing at hand.

6.   Focus on the task for as long as possible. Work in chunks, focus for as long as you can.

7.   Enjoy yourself. Turn achieving flow into a game and make the most of it.

8.   Practise. Practise makes perfect; don't expect full flow results immediately each and every time.

I hope to hear stories about you achieving flow. There is no feeling like it when it happens.

"Do not dwell in the past, do not dream of the future, concentrate the mind on the present moment."

Buddha

People / Employees

People are one of the biggest unknowns in business, and having employees is one of the biggest financial commitments and hassle you can have. Now I'm not saying you should avoid hiring people because no business can grow as a one-man band, but I am saying you should be careful who and how you hire.

If you are in an online business environment, there is no reason why you can't outsource all your staff on a month by month basis. I have so many full-time staff and they start out great, mostly working from home and then they end up slacking.

And remember this. No one is going to work as hard on your business as yourself. No one. There are things you can to provide incentive – for example, people appreciate profit shares etc. and this is a great thing to do.

Depending on where you are in the world, the employment laws are different from country to country too.

I know I don't like hiring people here in the UK; it's too much hassle and way too difficult to fire them if they are not what I want. I personally employ people on a contract basis. It may cost you more money each month, but the headaches associated with it are much less. Be careful who you hire and make sure they are the right people for the job. Having the wrong people working with you is the biggest killer of motivation and growth within a small organisation.

Outsourcing

I have hired tens of people to outsource my business to over the years and I have dealt with them directly. In fact, I needed an outsourcer to manage the outsourcers, which I thought at the time was the smart thing to do. It's not. My advice to you is to find a managed outsourcing company. I am just about to start working with one based in the Philippines, but Canadian people are running it and you deal with them. They deal with the outsourcers, hire the right people for your job and kick arse if things aren't getting done right. It may cost you 30% to 50% more to do it that way, but it's worth it in the long run, trust me.

To build your empire, you need to have people working for you. There are only so many hours in the day and no one can truly reach their full potential by only working on their own. Getting a right team of people behind you is the difference between only having a small business that pays your bills and a growing organisation that has the potential to change your life together with everyone who works with you. Outsourcing and delegation is the only way this can happen. Way too many times, I see people who are fearful of growing their business with people. These people spend way too much time working in their business and not working on their business. The way I managed to grow my adult site business so quickly was scaling it quickly. To do that, I hired good people who knew how to build systems and software to do that quickly. It was perfect, as we grew way too quickly to have a perfect system in place, but it did make money and it did sustain. Staff and people working with you is your decision to make, how many, who and where they are based etc. Ultimately if you want a lifestyle business that doesn't involve hiring anyone full-time to work with you, then that's fine, but if you want a business that eventually can run like a machine without you being there, you need to take to plunge and hire people to do things you don't like doing or you can pay less than your time is worth to. I say you should hire out anything you don't like doing as your days should eventually be full of things you like doing and are motivated to do . That way you will have the will and enthusiasm to make it happen rather than hating doing things. That's what people working with you are there to do.

Check out my links to the outsource companies I use in the life and business tools section in the website resources section.

I have struggled with hiring people and managing people; I'm a terrible manager of people. I am either too hard on them or too soft. I can't seem to get it right. Over the course of the coming months, I am going to be looking to hire a business manager that manages most people who work with me. For me, that cuts down the amount of management of people I have to do. I will only deal with the business manager and my PA on a daily basis.

Like I said at the beginning, people are one of the biggest unknowns in any business and, for an entrepreneur, finding good people to work for them is one of the biggest gambles around.

> ### *Marky's Tip -*
> *Don't sleep with anyone you hire. I did and although it was great at the time, it changes things. ;) Don't do it... I'm never hiring another PA that I am attracted to ever again. (Maybe more on that later if I decide to include it.)*

Online Business

I could write an entire book about online business. In fact, I will do some day. I have included as much information I can in the space I have to get you thinking about if an online business is for you. You may already have one, or may be thinking of setting up one.

Things online change all the time. It's so important to keep up with those changes in order to maximise your business and, ultimately, your profits too. For me, online business is the way forward. It's flexible, exciting, fast-moving and potentially very lucrative with low overheads.

It's a freedom thing

For me, working online mean freedom and flexibility to do what I want, when I want and to operate where I want. My friend, Mark Anastasi, wrote a book about living a 'Laptop Millionaire' lifestyle and it's a very real thing that hundreds of people do all of the time.

Running the porn sites meant I only needed a laptop and a mobile phone; it was great. I could be anywhere in the world and run everything. Many times I sat in The Bahamas and ran everything from paradise.

Not much has changed now apart from I spend more time in coffee shops than on beaches at the moment.

If you set up your online business correctly, you should be able to live a laptop lifestyle with ease. In many ways, the freedom it gives me makes me more productive than being stuck at one place. I would hate the thought of having to work in one place only. I have had offices before and I like having an office, but nothing beats getting the laptop and sitting out in the sun and working away.

Freedom is everything to me and being able to enjoy such a flexible daily routine is great.

Setting Up Online

As with anything, you should set up your online business correctly from the start. Spending extra time and, in some cases, more money from the get-go, means less hassles and problems later on.

Depending on the products you are going to sell, you only need the basics to set up your business: hosting, a domain name, an auto responder and maybe a shopping cart system. If you accept PayPal, you are in business within minutes too.

You're about to begin your journey into building a successful online business. As an online entrepreneur, you will be able to instantly tap into a global marketplace where you can build a brand, explore profitable markets and put yourself on the path towards financial freedom.

You've heard and seen the success stories online about how average, everyday people were able to go from nothing to building highly, profitable online businesses in a short amount of time. The greatest part of these success stories is that for many of these ordinary folks, they wouldn't have ever stood a chance of being successful had it not been for the Internet.

Think about it, where else can you tap into such an unlimited customer base?

Exciting stuff, isn't it? :)

What are you good at?

One of the easiest ways of deciding what kind of business you are going to set up is by asking yourself what you are good at. What skills or knowledge do you have that you could start an online business with? If you can develop a solid interest into online business, your learning curve will be greatly shortened.

Doing something you are good at and doing something that you love will make your online business set up much easier. For me, I am good at putting things together, having the vision to get them implemented, but I am no good at seeing the projects all the way through to the end; that's where I need other people to help me.

What wakes you up in the morning?

This has been a big thing for me. One of the things I have learned is that by having something that makes you want to get up in the morning, and if it is the first thing that you think about on waking, then you are more likely to be successful. I have two such things going on at the moment and it excites me. I love the feeling. There is no point setting up any business offline or online that doesn't excite you. What's the point?

You are going to be spending days, weeks and potentially years building this business; what's the point in not getting up on a Monday morning and WANTING to jump right on it?

Keeping it simple

One of the things I have always done in the past is to overcomplicate things. I am someone that naturally has tried without knowing it to overcomplicate things. Not for any other reason than thinking it needs to be like that to work. My advice when setting up or developing your existing online business is to keep things simple. This was proven only last week when my friend Brad and I sold one of our sites on flippa.com and we got over $15,000 from the sale. It was a simple site, simple product and we had some affiliates promote it. (It was a pack of over 250 exclusive tunes I had made myself.)

My advice is to keep all your products and services simple; make them great and people will buy them. Complicated puts customers off and complicated makes your job a hell of a lot harder too.

"Very narrow areas of expertise

can be very productive.

Develop your own profile.

Develop your own niche."

Leigh Steinberg

Target Markets

Before you can begin building your business, you need to know who your audience will be and what approach to take.

We figure this out through niche market research.

Don't let the word 'research' scare you off! It's an incredibly important step in the process of building a business geared for success. It's also a very easy step, and I'll show you exactly how I quickly evaluate different markets, including existing competition to determine whether a specific niche is viable or not.

To start, it's important that you understand exactly what a 'niche market' really is.

Niche marketing can be defined simply as: marketing a product or service that caters to a specific customer base.

Most mainstream niches will be very competitive, so it's often wise to chisel down into the niche so that you are targeting a subset group of buyers who are in a smaller segment of that niche.

Every niche market that you focus on should have an existing consumer base.

You don't want to spend the time, money or the legwork of creating a business from scratch in a new or untapped niche. Instead, focus your attention (and energy) on VERIFIED, PROVEN markets where you can instantly identify that there is a current demand for specific products and services.

Also, keep in mind that the more you know about a niche and its target audience, the easier it will be to develop products or services, or to promote campaigns so that they are communicating directly with your average customer.

Once you narrow down your niche, by analysing profitability, conducting market research and then determining the type of product or service that is likely to be successful based on what is already consistently selling, you can then rinse and repeat this system for each new market that you venture into.

This type of research, where you carve out a listing of profitable sub-niches, rather than focusing on the larger markets will automatically give you an advantage over those larger companies that generalise niches under one main category.

Here's why.

You can quickly become an expert in your niche by focusing on building your brand within one market at a time.

It's easier to keep current with a narrowly focused market niche than to cover all mainstream markets (and their sub-niches).

You can respond faster to changes in the market and adjust your marketing as new trends emerge.

You can build close relationships with key customers while avoiding the struggle of competing with established merchants who have already dominated (and saturated) the market.

Another reason why it's often more feasible to focus on smaller, sub-niche markets rather than broader mainstream ones is simply because of the extended opportunity to create new products that may not have been introduced to your target audience yet.

Sub-niches can be just as profitable as mainstream ones, even with fewer consumers. Focus on the markets with 'long-term growth', where you are able to develop future products and offer them to the same target consumer base.

When considering a niche, absorb EVERYTHING you can about it including:

1) Exactly what your potential customers are looking for or need help with

2) Where they currently go for help or advice

3) What types of products are they currently purchasing

4) Is there a desperate need for information products in this market?

5) Are these buyers likely to become repeat customers?

You want to look for a market that can be easily be targeted by a clear, identifiable problem, need or demand and fill in the gaps with an information product that offers this market a solution to their problems.

One thing to keep in mind is that when it comes to market evaluation, you are NOT just out to determine the size of the buyer's market.

While it's always important to verify that there is enough demand for products or services in any given niche, the easiest way to determine the potential of a market is by looking at the existing competition.

Think about it, the more competition targeting a specific niche, the more profitable it's likely to be, right? Otherwise, there wouldn't be as many competitors desperate to claim their place in the market.

But we also have to balance things out.

After all, we don't want to spend a lot of time and money trying to penetrate an overpopulated market where the competition is so incredibly stiff that we'd constantly struggle to secure even a tiny share of the marketplace.

Customers and List Building

Building a list of people and customers is one of the most important things you should be doing as soon as you can, no matter what business you have online. But I have learned many lessons about list building in the last three years. When I first started again in 2009, I heard about people having 100,000+ lists. I wanted one. I had plans to build my list of Internet Marketing subscribers to over 50,000 people as soon as I could.

Within a year, I had my 100,000 list and at the 12 month point, I made good money from it. As I speak, I have 220,000 people on my list. Making money from your list is powerful. Once you have a responsive list of customers, you should be looking to earn from them each month.

Let me tell you something about list building though...

The thing with list building is that it is not all in the size of your list!

THE MONEY IS IN THE LIST

People say that the money is in the list and, well, it is, but **it's more accurate to say the money is in the relationship you have with your list.** After all, there is no point in having a 220,000 person list if no one cares what you say on it and no one buys anything from you.

There is something else about list building too... I have learned that the **money is in the amount of value you give to your list.**

Simon Hodgkinson taught me this. I was looking to make a new website and was contemplating making it into a paid membership but Simon suggested that it should be free.

He told me that if he could have his time again, he would knock a lot of time off his business building if he had concentrated on giving his subscribers lots of value. Give them something for a month and they will buy from you, in fact, they will want to buy.

It's true... give as much value to your list as you can and they will thank you for it.

Every single day, I uploaded a new product to the site. This meant that each day, all of my subscribers on the mailing list received an update from me, telling them I'm giving them something else for free. It's a powerful long-term game plan.

Find something to give away within your niche and start list building. You can find free squeeze page templates if you Google 'free squeeze page templates'.

Here is the biggest lesson I can teach you about List Building:

BUILD A LIST OF CUSTOMER AS QUICK AS YOU CAN!!!

People that have actually paid you for products are far more valuable to you than a list of freebie seekers. I would much rather have a 1,000 customer list than 200,000 people on a list who have never paid me a penny.

A buyer is far more valuable than a freebie seeker.

List size means nothing... buyer list sizes means everything...

Auto responders

To build your lists and to manage your customers quickly and easily, you need to automate much of the process. Auto responders should be a key element in any online business. You need to sign up to one to be able to control and manage all your email lists and customer lists.

I use two auto responders at the moment. Most of my email is going into GetResponse.com which I find slightly easier to use than AWeber.com but AWeber.com does have some features that are not contained in Get Response.

Both companies charge roughly the same amount per month (about $18 per month for up to 500 subscribers).

I like the layout of GetResponse.com - but AWeber.com has some features that Get Response doesn't. For instance, you can email all the people that didn't open a previous email without emailing the people that did. Check both companies out and decide for yourself which one is best for you. :)

Another company I use is ImnicaMail.com - check it out for a great alternative to the main two companies.

Building the Relationship with your List

When it comes to list building, it is critical that every email you send out to your subscriber base is audited against your brand personality and that you are accurately reflecting your brand. Build a trusting relationship with your subscriber base and ultimately, nurture your list so that they are conditioned to respond to your offers, whether they are free or promotional-based.

You want people to trust you and to ultimately look to you for advice and help with their problems. You also want to ensure that your emails compliment and improve brand awareness as it will have a DIRECT impact on your ability to monetise your mailings.

Imagine having thousands of subscribers interested in your broadcasts, anxious to read your emails and loyal to following your updates.

Think about the potential if your response rate was steadily high every time you sent out a broadcast, promoting products and services that you believe would directly help your subscriber base in some way.

If you put the time and effort into growing and nurturing your list, you can ultimately make more money from a single broadcast then through nearly ANY other form of marketing. One email – one click = payday.

But it all hinges on your ability and dedication to building a relationship with each and every subscriber. You want your emails to speak directly to them, to communicate a clear message and to work towards building trust and loyalty.

This means that before you begin sending promotional broadcasts to your subscriber base, you need to conduct market research and effectively evaluate what your target market is looking for and how to deliver it to them.

Once you've done that, you need to spend time over creating and delivering high quality content, material and resources to win them over and establish that important credibility.

When it comes to building a relationship with your list, there is ultimately one method that works better than all others: Offering VALUABLE content.

Hands down, it's by the far the easiest way to win their trust and establish yourself as a credible source of information or an authority on your topic. Yet few email marketers make this a priority and instead focus more on the quantity of their newsletters and broadcasts than the overall quality.

People need time to develop a rapport with you based on trust and on direct experience with dealing with you, and via regular and consistent communication before they are likely to buy from you. You can begin building these blocks of trust by over delivering on high quality, valuable and free content.

Courting subscribers is a term that describes the process of building relationships with your lists and prospects. You need to take your time with this process, and put the effort into building your reputation as someone who is worth listening to.

This doesn't happen overnight, but if you work on it every day, before too long, your list will be an exceptionally responsive one.

Here are some tips to establishing credibility and building the best possible relationships with your subscribers:

Always follow through

If you ever make an offer to your list, make sure that you are able to follow through on your promises. Whether you are offering free content or a paid one, it doesn't matter. You need to follow through and deliver what you say you will.

Always follow up

Don't ever let your list run cold through a lack of communication. If you are concerned about 'over emailing' your list, keep in mind that you can email your list as frequently as you wish if you are offering solid, useful content.

Conduct surveys and request feedback

Your subscribers will ultimately become your most valuable business asset and you need to value each and every one of them. While it's impossible to always please everyone, if you are putting an effort into concisely targeting your subscriber base so that you are focusing on providing relevant, strong content, you will be able to successfully build your business all from your email marketing campaigns.

Maintain consistency

Part of the relationship building process involves the frequency in which you email your list. If you only email your list once a quarter or just a few times every few months, odds are that you will experience a large number of bounce rates. People are likely to unsubscribe from your list simply because they don't remember who you are, what your brand is or possibly even why they signed up in the first place. Staying in frequent communication with your subscribers is a critical element to your email marketing success' just be sure that each time you do send out a broadcast or mailing that you are offering something of exceptional value.

*"Everyone lives by
selling something."*

Robert Louis Stevenson

Products

I f you run an online business, you only normally make any money when you sell products. For this reason, you MUST have your own products.

If you want to make any serious money online, you have got to develop your own products. Right from the get-go, I started developing my own products. I talk about how you can make a lot of money out of affiliate promotions in the next chapter. I do think affiliate promotion is great. There is a difference with the way I did it though.

I created membership sites. If I had wanted to, I could have turned the membership sites into my own sites using my own credit card processing or I could have moved them to another affiliate system. In my opinion, you need to create your own products and do affiliate promotion too. You need to learn how to start creating products as fast as you can. I have suffered from trying too hard with product creation, and making sure every little thing is taken care of. I have learned to stop doing that... well, most of the time.

You need to learn how to create a product and get it out there as soon as possible. I have some big resources online for helping you to create products. Check them out at the end of the book.

Pre-made content

Pre-made content is available in many markets and it offers a quick and effective way to get started while you are creating your own products. You should become familiar with specific terms and licenses relating to **pre-made content** that is available for purchase.

With ready-made content, you can use it to power up your websites, add content to new blogs, use in auto responder campaigns or even in affiliate marketing. In fact, there are also certain types of content releases that will even allow you to rebrand as your own!

Pre-made content is broken down into three distinct groups or categories:

Resell rights

When you purchase a product that provides resell rights, it means that you can sell the product on your own website, but cannot claim ownership or modify it to include your name.

While Resell Rights are often more affordable than other options, if you want to establish your own brand online, it's never the best way to go.

Private label rights

With private label rights (known as PLR), you are able to edit the document however you like, and can add your name to it.

Sometimes PLR includes the ability to pass rights onto your customers as well, although you do want to pay close attention to how limited the PLR is, since the fewer that are able to purchase it, the more the quality will be retained.

Master resell rights

With master resell rights (MRR), you are able to sell the product on your website, and also pass along the rights to sell it to others. You cannot add your name to the document, and most often you are not provided with the source (DOC file).

Whenever you do purchase a product with any kind of rights, try to acquire a 'license' document that details what is permitted, so that in the event you are asked to show that you have rights to sell or distribute the document, you are able to do so.

If you are unclear about what certain rights apply, or what they mean, you should always contact the product author (original owner) and to have them clarified before you begin selling it on your website.

Regardless of what direction you choose to take, whether you have decided to build a business as an affiliate marketer or as a product developer yourself, I'll show you how to quickly set up your online business with the essential tools of the trade in the next chapter.

*"Affiliate Marketing has
made businesses millions
and ordinary people millionaires.
Affiliate Marketing
may be your next
best career move."*

Larry Bussey

Your Own Affiliate Programme

One of the easiest ways of jump-starting your online business is by building an army of affiliates who will spread your message, promote your products and, ultimately, maximise your exposure in a greater way than you are likely ever to be able to do on your own.

When it comes to building an affiliate programme, you aren't required to install or configure scripts, nor must you invest in expensive affiliate software. Instead, you can begin exposing your business to a network of affiliates just by adding your product to JVZoo.com. I love JVZoo and the guys that run it; it is a sophisticated yet simple to use PayPal-based affiliate programme and marketplace. Check them out at http://marklyford.com/likes/jvzoo.

If you are interested in running your own "in-house" affiliate programme, I recommend OfficeAutoPilot as it is flexible, customisable and affordable. Plus it simplifies the process of managing and paying affiliates. Check out http://marklyford.com/likes/oap for more details.

Apart from listing your product in online marketplaces like JVZoo, however, you have to be proactive in actually RECRUITING affiliates. Don't expect that just by showcasing your product via the JVZoo marketplace that affiliates will instantly begin promoting you. While it's likely that a handful of affiliates will pick it up, you have to do your part to provide them with a clear incentive.

Why should they promote YOUR products, rather than someone else's?

You need to therefore focus on the affiliate's individual benefits.

While it's important to assure potential affiliates that your product is of high quality, refunds are low and you are available for ongoing support, you also have to take other things into account. This includes the actual commission percentage that you are awarding affiliates, as well as the promotional material that you have readily available to help them promote you.

You need to make things as easy on your affiliates as possible, and the more effort you put into developing detailed affiliate creative and promotional pages (including various landing pages, article content and even free reports that affiliates can use to warm up their lists), the more likely affiliates will respond to your offer.

You want them to be able to start promoting you instantly, without having to develop promotional material themselves.

Make sure that you create a ready-made promotional page on your website that offers a variety of promotional banners (in various sizes) as well as additional tools that they can use to reach out to their subscribers and leads.

Here are a few things to keep in mind when developing your affiliate programme:

Payouts – Affiliates want high payouts, they want to be paid often, they want to be paid by their favourite payout method, and they want to be paid on time every single time with no delays, no excuses and no hassles.

They don't want to have to fill out forms, request payment manually or set up accounts apart from the ones they currently use, such as PayPal. In other words, they want to be able to receive their earnings easily, without jumping through hoops.

Bonuses – Affiliates love bonuses and rewards. Incentives can be incredible motivators. Not only can they help attract new affiliates to your programme and get them promoting you, but if you offer really great incentives, it can even motivate them to work harder overall!

Contests – Affiliates absolutely love contests and competitions. Being able to earn gifts, products or cash is a great way to boost up activity and jump-start your affiliate campaign. If you go a step further and publish the results on a hidden 'Affiliates Only' page that showcases your top affiliates, you will see the competition shift up a notch or two, as affiliates try to outsell and outperform one another just to be listed and ranked on your page.

Promotional material – Affiliates want promotional material. You need to offer them as much promotional material as possible in order to make their job in promoting your programme as easy as possible.

The more promotional material, the better – you can NEVER go overboard and, if you can go a step further and offer blog posts, auto responder message sequences that they can use to send to their list, pre-made templates and anything else you can think of, the easier your programme will be to promote.

Banners sizes to consider: You should have at least two or three of each common size. Some great sizes to include are 468x60, 234x60, 468x80, 88x31, 120x60, 120x240, 125x90, 125x125, 150x150, 300x250, 728x90, 120x600 and 160x600.

Pop-up ads, pop under ads, floating ads etc. You can offer plain text and graphically enhanced versions and include instructions for affiliates to include them on their pages. You can hire a programmer to create the code for these, if needed, but there are many programs and WordPress plug-ins that do this quickly and easily for you. Pop-up ads are a pain sometimes if you are a surfer but the reality is they work and bring more money in than not using them.

Promotional articles that relate to your product. For example, if your product is a weight-loss eBook, you could offer some free PLR articles offering simple tips for raising your metabolism, simple exercises, how to decrease your appetite, how to stay motivated on a diet, etc.

Easy equates to productive, especially when it comes to affiliate marketing. You want to give them every reason imaginable to promote your product so, by decreasing the workload and giving them 'ready-made' material, you will encourage activity!

Aside from your actual affiliate offer, you also want to make sure that your website and product are polished and presentable. Affiliates want to promote high quality content, well-designed websites and products that impress.

They're working hard to promote you and, in exchange, they want low refund requests, prompt customer support and to see that you've done your job at building trust on your sales page and in taking care of customers once they've directed them to your site.

You should also consider offering a review copy of your product to qualified affiliates who are interested in previewing your information prior to promoting you.

While you don't have to offer a free copy to everyone, established affiliates have earned the right to be particular with the products and services that they promote, and it's reasonable for them to request a personal copy.

If you have any kind of online business, you should have an affiliate programme. It's all about leverage and scale; having affiliates that send you sales in exchange for a percentage of the profits is the way many online businesses have grown quickly. Don't have an affiliate programme? Get one now.

> *Marky's Thought -*
> *I would rather make 50% off lots of sales than*
> *100% off fuck all ;)*

"Quality in a service or product is not what you put into it. It is what the client or customer gets out of it."

Peter Drucker

Making Money As An Affiliate

I have made over $30,000 a month in just affiliate promotions in the past. It's a great way to make money. In order to be successful in affiliate marketing, you have to choose the products you intend to promote just as carefully as you choose the keywords that you use to optimise your website for the search engines.

When it comes to affiliate marketing, successful marketers know that in order to stand out from the crowd they have to:

1) Choose high converting, quality products

2) Add value to their campaigns

3) Go above the call of duty and over deliver to potential customers

When evaluating potential products, there are a few things to keep in mind, primarily, how well the product is converting, whether the developer has done their part in creating a compelling sales page (based on conversion rates) and what commissions and incentives are being offered to affiliates.

You also want to base your decision around existing competition, whether the market is penetrable or if you'd struggle to generate leads based on an overload of competition already solidified in the marketplace.

When evaluating potential products within the JVZoo marketplace, you are given statistical data that will help you determine the profitability (and popularity) of any given product.

The best place to start to do this is: http://www.jvzoo.com/products/topsellers

There you will be able to see and search for the best-selling products, by launch date, amount sold, conversion rates and more.

You will also see the amount of units each product has sold, with the commission paid to affiliates, the $ per sale and the refund rate too.

Paying attention to the EPC (earnings per click) is also important as it indicates how much you will receive each time you generate a successful sale. The EPC is similar as it indicates the commission percentage awarded.

Finding solid products to promote is relatively easy, but in order to convert traffic into buyers through your affiliate link, you need to put a bit more effort into the way you present your campaigns.

This is where 'Added Value' comes into play.

You've probably seen marketers offering incentives, including bonus products, discounts on additional products or services, or freebies in exchange for buying a product through their affiliate link. This works (and works very well) because what it does is to target leads that are already on the verge of buying, and to give them the push they need to make the sale.

You can add value to your affiliate campaigns in a number of different ways, including:

1) Offering additional components that add value to the core product

This is where you would create extended training, tools or resources that compliment and expand on the main product you are trying to sell.

For example, if you were promoting a course on Niche Marketing, you could offer a bonus package that included a 'Niche Swipe File', video training helping people survey and evaluate niche markets, or additional guides and resources that help to expand, clarify or to explain the information within the course.

2) Offering additional products or services

This is similar to creating components for the product, but instead of offering information or tools that expand on the specific product, you could consider offering other products (related to the topic, but not directly connected to the product you are promoting).

For example, if you were promoting a guide on 'profitable blogging', you could offer potential customers a premium WordPress theme package for buying through your link.

3)   Develop a USP

You want to stand out from the hundreds of other offers that your leads are most likely receiving (and potentially growing immune to). To do this, you need a unique selling proposition (USP) with every affiliate promotion, which is all about showcasing your offers value so that it stands above and beyond everyone else's.

You want people to see your offer as more valuable and to feel that they are gaining MORE by purchasing through your affiliate link. This is absolutely vital for being able to clearly distinguish your offer from your competitors.

Your offer needs to be unique, feature a specific benefit and to be compelling enough to motivate people to buy from you.

Here are a few ideas on creating your own USP:

Offer ongoing support

Many affiliate marketers are focused only on the immediate sale and you can use this to your advantage. Offer customers ongoing support after the sale. Not only will this help to eliminate any concerns that potential customers may have, but it is likely to result in repeat sales through future campaigns.

Offer free bonuses, incentives, gifts, products, certificates

Try to offer something unique, even if you have to create it yourself (or hire a freelancer to develop it for you). The more valuable and original your offer, the easier it will be to convince potential buyers that your offer is the best one.

Study the competition, determine what they are offering and consider how you can offer a more valuable incentive offer. Fill in the gaps, go the extra mile and brainstorm for ways that you can set yourself and your offer apart. A little bit of extra effort will go a long, long, way.

> ### Marky's Thought -
> *Being an affiliate eliminates the hassles of product creation but you are giving away your customer list by doing it. The ideal way is to have enough customers coming in and a combination of your own products and to be an affiliate for only the best products.*

Info publishing

Selling information products is about the best thing you can do to get started online. But be warned from the get-go; don't just jump into selling information products on how to make money. It's not the way to do it.

What Should You Sell?

If you're an information seller, then you already know that there are plenty of ways to package your information. The decision of how to present your information depends on a variety of factors, including but not limited to:

- What your market wants and responds to

- Pricing considerations: Certain packaging increases perceived value and allows you to charge more

- The information itself – some information may be better suited to videos, some are better suited to text, and so on

- Whether you want to offer a downloadable product, a shipped product, or a hybrid product

When you take the above factors into consideration, here are the primary packaging choices you have:

- **Downloadable Reports and eBooks:** Some people use these terms interchangeably. However, reports are generally shorter than eBooks. Nonetheless, both tend to be in the lower price range of information products as they have a lower perceived value.

- **eCourses:** Generally eCourses are delivered by email in multiple parts over multiple days. Like eBooks and reports, eCourses tend to be on the lower end of the price range. However, if you spread the lessons out over several months, you can charge per month, thus earning at least temporary residual income.

- **Memberships and Recurring Products:** These fall under the 'forced continuity' category, where members are automatically re-billed (like web hosting or the 'fruit of the month' club). The month-to-month charge tends to be low – about the price of an eBook – but the value of the customer is higher since it's a recurring charge.

- **High-end Intermediate Courses:** These sorts of courses may be delivered in a variety of formats. In this case, it's the information itself and not the format that most impacts the perceived value. Since these are intermediate courses, their actual prices start at mid-range and go up.

- **Audio Products:** Audio products have a higher perceived value because of the unique format. You can further increase the value by including the transcripts. Top dollar comes into play when you offer admission to live audio events, such as teleconferences.

- **Video Products:** Like audio products, videos have a higher perceived value. As such, you may be able to charge more than you would for traditional text, just because of the format. However, this is only true if the content is improved by putting it into video format. You'll do yourself no favours if you use videos when text would work just as well. For example, offering a simple PowerPoint type presentation may frustrate customers who'd rather just read the text at their own pace. On the other hand, a recorded workshop is a good use of video.

- **'Big Package' Products:** Typically, these are physical products that are shipped and arrive in a big box, thereby hitting the customer with the 'thud' factor. Because there are an almost-overwhelming number of books, DVDs, and/or CDs arriving, the package tends to have a higher perceived value. Generally, these big package products start at around $500 and easily go into four figures.

- **High-Ticket Training:** These products are $1,000 and up, and usually involve live events like weekend seminars. The benefit of offering information in this form is that you can charge both for the live event as well as the DVD recordings.

- **Personal One-on-One Training:** Information packaged in the form of personal consulting or coaching commands the highest price due to the personal attention. Often those who purchase high-ticket workshops go on to purchase personal consultations. The prices are almost always four figure prices, but can easily reach five figures.

As you've seen on the previous pages, **both the format as well as the content itself determines price.**

However, there's one other thing you may want to take into consideration. Namely, physical products tend to have lower refund rates. As such, overall you may find higher profits since fewer people ask for refunds.

The most probable reason for the refund rate difference is that physical products require the customer to do some 'work' to get their refund. Whereas a digital product just requires an email to the creator, a physical product needs to be repackaged and shipped back to the creator in order to get a refund.

As such, many product creators opt for **hybrid products that are part-downloadable, partly-shipped physical product.**

The downloadable portions of the product allow the customer some instant gratification, while the fact that is part-physical lowers refund rates. In addition, since the hybrid product is a part-physical product, it has a higher perceived value.

There are other disadvantages to both physical and digital products.

Digital products have security problems, in that you're more likely to see your product being illegally shared and even pirated. On the flip side, having a physical product means you need to deal with duplication and distribution issues.

Neither format is perfect. Instead, choose the one that is best suited to your business.

Creating the product

In general, there are three approaches you can use to create your product.

You may even choose to use these approaches together to create your product. Let's look at each method:

1. Do it yourself

Creating a product yourself isn't for everyone. However, you might consider doing it yourself if one or more of the following applies to you:

- You're an expert on the topic.

- You have a strong interest in the topic.

- Your strengths include research and quality content creation. (In other words, if you're a good writer and you intend to create an eBook, then doing it yourself may be right for you.)

The above are the most common reasons why you might create the product yourself. However, you might also choose to do so if you have more time than money, as might be the case if you're just starting out. If money isn't an issue, then instead you may choose to outsource your product creation.

2.   Outsource your product creation

If you're not an expert on the topic and/or you don't have a strong interest in it, then there's probably no advantage to you creating the product yourself.

Instead, **you can turn it over to a trusted freelancer to create it for you.**

They'll do just as good of job as you in researching and writing the content... and in fact, they'll probably create a better eBook than you could have written yourself.

There are other advantages to this method...

- Hiring a freelancer to complete the product **frees up your time for more important matters**, such as creating your marketing campaign and planning what other products to put into your sales funnel.

- When you give the product creation to someone else, **you speed up the entire process since you're free to focus on other issues**. That means you can bring products to market much more quickly than if you were trying to do everything yourself.

- Hiring a freelancer **may actually turn out to be cheaper than doing it yourself**. To figure out if this is true for you, start by putting a value on your time. Then figure out how many hours it would take you to complete a task. Multiply that by the value you put on an hour of your time. Then compare that to the price of hiring a freelancer.

For example, let's suppose you place a value of $50 per hour on your time. And let's suppose a particular project would take you 40 hours to complete. Take 40 hours X $50 per hour = $2,000. If a freelancer charges anything less than $2,000 to complete the same task, then it may be wiser for you to hire a freelancer.

If you decide that it would be wise to hire a freelancer, where should you look for someone reliable?

Ideally you should get a direct recommendation from someone you know and trust. If your friends can't give you any specific recommendations, then visit a business and marketing forum where you know and trust several of the members. Ask for recommendations, and pay attention to who is giving you the recommendations.

If you don't go that route, another way to find a freelancer is to visit freelancing sites like the popular Elance.com. Always be sure to check the freelancer's feedback on the site to ensure they have a long history and a good reputation for quality work.

Finally, you can simply search online for the type of freelancer you want, such as 'ghostwriter' or 'freelance programmer'.

Regardless of how you find your freelancer, **be sure to do your due diligence first.**

Search for the person's name, company name, and domain name online to see if you can uncover their history. You're looking for someone with a long history and good reputation. Be sure to also check references, as well as asking your colleagues if they know anything about the freelancer.

3. Recruit joint venture partners to create the product

Finally, you can create a product by recruiting **experts in the market to contribute to the product.**

This results in a product that's co-created by some of the biggest names in your market, **which lends instant credibility to the product – and to you.** Another advantage is that often your co-creators will also help you market the product.

As you might expect, this is a particularly good method to choose if you're just entering a niche.

Building familiarity and trust as well as establishing yourself as a credible expert are things you must do in any niche when you're just starting out. This may take many months or even years to do.

However, **when you join forces with established experts, you get to borrow their credibility,** which means you're almost instantly established in the niche as an expert. From there, you can go on to sell more products to your newfound customer base.

You can see why this approach is a good way to establish yourself in a niche as an expert. But how do you create a product in this way?

The first thing you need to do is decide in which format you're going to present your product. Obviously this will depend on which format your niche prefers, such as audio over text.

Secondly, however, you must also take into consideration your joint venture partners' busy schedules.

You see, asking someone to write answers to interview questions, or to write an article, may be deemed as more work than getting on the phone and doing a quick interview.

On the flip side, you may be dealing with experts who haven't done much in the way of teleconferences, and are thus a little hesitant to speak live to their market.

In order to determine what is best for your joint venture partners, **ask them which they prefer.**

You may end up doing a product that's part-audio and part-text... and that's ok. Or you may be able to convince those who are partial to writing an article for an eBook to do a teleconference instead, especially if their colleagues have already agreed to get on the phone with you.

In addition, you can also look around your niche and see what types of products these marketers are already putting out. If they're all selling audio, then you know that they're comfortable doing teleconferences... and you know the market is comfortable buying them.

Regardless of what type of product you choose to create, your job is to make it as easy as possible for your joint venture partners to do their part:

- If you're asking them to submit a contribution to an eBook, then ask them for something short and sweet, like a 1,000 word article.

- If you're asking them to get on the phone to do an interview with you, then prepare them ahead of time by giving them an outline of questions you might ask. In addition, you may want to talk to them a day or two ahead of time so they can become comfortable with you. Your job is to make them feel relaxed and prepared for the interview.

- If you're asking your partners to speak at a live event, such as a weekend workshop, then again do everything you can to help them. That includes making their travel arrangements, if necessary.

In other words, you want your joint venture partners to do as little as possible, and yet get as much benefit as possible. This will make it more likely that they will say yes to your request. Keep in mind that most experts get dozens of similar request every week, so anything that looks easy and yet provides a decent return on their investment of time will likely interest them.

Note: The benefit that you're offering to prospective joint venture partners is exposure and back-end income opportunities. If you're creating an eBook with these partners, then give them a resource box to promote themselves. If you're doing audio events or workshops, then allow them to pitch their products at the end of the interview.

Note, however, that you can also request to use YOUR affiliate link in the resource box or at the end of a live event. This way, you can both benefit from the exposure.

Finally, one of the benefits of using joint venture partners to help create your product is that it does tend to be quicker than doing it yourself. However, you'll need an additional skill set to pursue this method, such as the ability to manage projects and people, as well as the ability to persuade people to work on your project with you.

Summary

So which product creation method is right for you? As you've discovered, it all depends on a variety of factors. These factors include, but are not limited to:

- Whether you're already established in a niche, or if you need a little help getting established

- Whether you have more time or money

- Whether or not you're an expert in the field

- Whether or not you have a strong interest in the topic

- Your ability to manage people and projects, as well as your ability to 'sell' people on your ideas

- Your patience and ability to do the 'due diligence' that's necessary to hire freelancers or work with joint venture partners.

- Whether or not there's any advantage to you personally creating the product, as the case might be if it's shown that your market wants you to create a workshop or teleconference on the topic. (In which case, hiring a ghostwriter to write an eBook just won't work.)

There is no right or wrong answer here. Indeed, you may use different methods for different products.

For example, you may create your entry-level product yourself, but you may recruit joint venture partners to help you create part of your 'big package' product. Indeed, you may create part of the product yourself, and have the other half created by freelancers or your partners.

Again, there's no 'one size fits all' solution... rather you should look at your individual situation, and choose the best solution for the particular product you're creating.

Product pricing techniques

How much should you charge for your product?

Here are the steps to take to help you make that decision:

1.   Look at similar products

You've already analysed the competition and have noted what they're charging for their content. If most of the similar products in your niche all charge around the same amount, that gives you a good place to start.

However, keep this in mind...

2.   Format affects prices

As discussed at the beginning of this report, different formats carry different perceived values.

For example, a live event such as a teleconference is generally perceived as more valuable than an eBook. Physical products that are shipped to the customer's door tend to be perceived as more valuable than downloadable products.

Check out what format your competitors are using, and how they're delivering their content.

If your competitors offer downloadable eBooks, you can offer very similar information for around the same price that they charge. However, change the format into a physical product or perhaps an audio or video product, and you can charge more for your product.

3.   Once you have a ballpark figure, start testing prices

You can sit around all day long and try to guess which price will result in the most overall profit for you. However, the only way to tell for sure is to let your customers vote with their wallets. This means split testing your different prices to ascertain which one provides the best results.

When it comes to pricing, don't make any assumptions.

While you may assume that a lower price will result in higher conversions being achieved, that's not always true. Indeed, you may be pleasantly surprised to find that the higher your price, the better your overall profit – meaning conversions are higher and refunds are lower.

While this seems counterintuitive, it makes sense when you think it through.

In essence, **when you raise your price, you also raise the perceived value of the product.**

The more valuable a product is, the more people want it – thus the increase in conversions. Because high-ticket buyers also tend to be more serious, if you're putting out a good product you may also see the added benefit of fewer refunds when you raise the price.

I mention this to you so that you're not afraid to raise your prices on your products.

However, remember that whether you raise or lower prices, you should always test them so you know how (and if) the changes are affecting your conversion rates.

How are they delivering their content – download, shipped, hybrid?

How much are they charging for their information?

What will your unique selling proposition be for your product?

Something I am moving into is WordPress development and software. I love software because it has the potential to cross many markets if you produce it and promote it correctly.

I hope after reading this chapter you realise how having information-based digital products can be lucrative. The great thing about it is you produce it once and you can sell as many copies of the same thing as you want.

> *Marky's Thought -*
> *Start with digital products and software. The overheads are low and the start-up costs can be as low as you need.*

Lifestyle Businesses

I f you are starting a business, you need to decide what kind of business it is going to be. Are you planning a business with the aim of it becoming substantial with people working for you, or do you want a lifestyle business?

A lifestyle business is one where you have more time to do what you want to do, but inevitably will not achieve massive financial success. (Unless you are really lucky.) Personally I have always wanted to build businesses that have massive potential, although I guess in my times of doubt I have thought to myself that a business that pays enough for me to not be stressed by money and gives me time to do other things would be nice. But it's just not me. As my friend Brad Gosse says, I'm the kind of person that goes 'balls deep' into something. And you know why? Because I only try and do things that motivate me. So for me, I don't view it as a chore, I view it as a challenge and a part of my life.

All of this comes down to what you want your life to be like on a daily, weekly or monthly basis. Only you can decide.

- Employment = Work for a set rate, little hassles, free time, leave your work at the office, have a definite divide

- Self-Employed = Free to do what you want to do to a point, work your own hours, but still swap time for money

- Lifestyle Business = set up a lifestyle business that may have other people working for you but the focus is on the lifestyle and not necessary the numbers and the cash

- Business = Grow, build and make a business thrive with other people helping you to build it. The sky is the limit with hard work

- Investor = Invest in other people's businesses.

Ultimately I wasn't into business and investments personally, but everyone is different, so make your own choice.

> ***Marky's Thought -***
>
> ***If it isn't worth doing right, don't do it at all.***

Exciting times

For me, there has never been a more exciting time to be online and to be involved with the Internet than right now. When I think back to how excited I was back in 1997 when I sent my first email, or how I was when I first surfed on a 100MB link at my web hosts, to think I now have 100MB in my house! How things have changed. I had the vision to know how things were going to be, but I didn't realise how fast things would move, I guess.

An online business levels the playing field. You can make a fortune if you get the right thing and there is no reason why you shouldn't be able to.

As you know from reading this book, I have run companies that have made, and lost, millions. And you know what? I probably will again.

I don't think I have been so excited about my online business future since first knowing I could make millions within the adult industry. I see people turning over millions with WordPress businesses and I know there are millions to be made in the coming years from crypto currencies like Bitcoin.

It's easy to keep up with what I am into and doing any particular day. I live my life on twitter at http://www.marklyford.com/twitter

Welcome to the digital party; let's grab a drink and make some money ;)

*"You must consider
the bottom line,
but make it integrity
before profits."*

Denis Waitley

Offline Businesses

I have had my fair share of offline bricks and mortar businesses. I have owned racing pigeon businesses, car valet companies, pawnbroker shops, to name but a few. I know many, many successful people who have offline businesses. So I am not saying I don't like operating an offline business.

One day I will have my own bar and I would always consider getting involved in any offline business that shows potential. One offline business I am particularly interested in is the storage industry; I like the low staff overheads of it but the thing that worries me about many offline businesses is the following:

Overheads

Overheads for offline businesses are typically far more than operating an online business (unless you are Google).

Now there are many markets for fusing offline and online business together, and that is one of the things I do; help offline businesses get online and to become profitable. One of the pending plans is to take online information products into the print / direct mail markets.

If you have an existing offline business, you need to get it online. I have yet to find a business that cannot make money by putting itself online. If you are considering setting up an offline business, really think hard about how you are going to utilise all the online business options available to you.

Just my two cents on offline businesses for you. :)

Smile - and be grateful

Prison did a great thing for me. It made me grateful for some of the more simple things in life. It takes fewer muscles to smile than it does to frown so I try and smile more these days.

I am incredibly grateful for the things in my life now, far more than I used to be. I appreciate the simple things as well as the cool things in life.

Try smiling when you feel pissed off or down and, for fuck sake, appreciate the things you have in life. I know if you suffer with depression nothing can change your mind at the time. But I try my hardest to just smile and say, "Fuck it!"

I don't do it enough and have to pull myself back and realise what I have in life sometimes. Being grateful for what you have in life will change your entire mindset very quickly.

Just try it now; smile and think of five things that you are grateful for in life. It will make you feel better, I promise.

The Future

For me, the future is an exciting place. Personally, I am looking forward to watching my two boys grow up into young men. I am looking forward one day to building the house I want in the UK and travelling a lot more too. I know, when the time is right, I will meet the love of my life too.

Businesswise, I am super excited about the future. After a year of massive changes for me in my business and a big shift in my thoughts towards my online activities, I now have a plan set.

My plans include setting up a new WordPress-based business, developing a training company for businesses and the biggest most exciting one of all are my new Bitcoin-based enterprises. In addition to this, I have a bunch of smaller one-off projects that I am planning throughout the next 12 months. So I am busy, which is how I love to be. I love the feeling of having exciting projects that wake me up in the morning, so that I can't wait to get out of bed and to get on.

Five years' time

In five years' time, I envisage having the above businesses established and going well. Everything changes all the time, of course, and, knowing me, I will have other things that I haven't even thought of going on too. That's being an entrepreneur though. :)

Personally, I hope to be living in my dream house in the UK on top of a hill, and to have a place somewhere in the sun that I can go to when the weather is bad here in the UK. It's fair to say the last 10 years have been massively up and down and I'm going to do everything I can to ensure the next 10 years are only full of ups, with just the occasional bump in the road (which is inevitable if you are as eager as I am to develop my life and that of my family too).

If you have read this far, it means you are serious about your life too. Congratulations. Just take a moment to think where you would like to be in five years' time and then commit to making it happen.

I hope we can all look back in five years' time with joy and see how far we have all come in the forthcoming chapters of our lives.

I hope this book has helped you with your life plans and enabled you to determine the direction that you would like to go in.

Just remember:

LIFE IS A GAME

And your happiness keeps the score.

And if you are an entrepreneur

BUSINESS IS A GAME

Money just keeps the score ;)

Have a life of fun, love, joy and happiness, and make sure you can look back and know that you have lived life to the full.

Now go and get to it!

Remember: Live the life you want, nothing else matters.

"Nothing can stop the man
with the right mental attitude
from achieving his goal;
nothing on earth
can help the man
with the wrong mental attitude."

Thomas Jefferson

It's Up To You

At the end of the day life, business, your attitude to life and how you deal with it, is up to you. You already know no one is going to give you everything you want on a plate. So, what are you going to do?

Being a rebel entrepreneur is about just going out to breaking rules. It's about saying a big, "Fuck you!" to what people think you should do, and doing what you want to do, what feels right for you.

How many years do you have left on this earth? How are you going to make those years count? What are you going to be remembered for?

The more you help people, the more the universe will give back to you. That's what I intend to do. I want to be remembered for helping people as much as possible. And not just from a business perspective. I have a lot to offer people, and so do you. Each and every one of us has our own set of unique qualities that can help people. I think that's what we are on earth to do.

All that matters is that you are remembered for something after you are gone, and remembered for something that you want to be remember for, not just someone who fitted in and did what was expected of them. Think about it; what a waste that would be.

I help to grow a group of people, where I can help in their business and their mindset. One thing I can do well is motivate people and if I inspire just a few people in the world after reading this book, then that's good enough for me.

Ask yourself, what's the one thing you will take away from reading this book? There will be hundreds of answers from hundreds of different people, but all that matters is what you take from it. I hope you take something positive and can go with that thought and turn it into something long-lasting and worthwhile for you.

Rebel against convention, rebel against popular thinking, rebel against life. Why would you? It's your own life and no one else's. ;)

Quotes

I love quotes. Reading good quotes has become a passion of mine. Over the years, I have read many, many books and pulled various thought-provoking things from them. I think quotes can be motivational and inspirational, and I have included some of my favourites throughout this book.

I thought I would share some more with you here.

"No idea is so outlandish that it should not be considered with a searching but at the same time a steady eye." – Winston Churchill

"People with goals succeed because they know where they are going .... It's as simple as that." – Earl Nightingale

"Courage is what it takes to stand up and speak; courage is also what it takes to sit down and listen." – Winston Churchill

"Remember the best way to increase your net worth is to increase your network." – Nigel Risner

"One of the greatest gifts you can give to anyone is the gift of attention." – Jim Rohn

"People don't care how much you know until they know how much you care." – Unknown

"What you do now creates your future."– Dr Joe Vitale

"The past is a place of reference, not a place of residency." – Willie Jollie

"We think much more about the use of our money, which is renewable, than we do about the use of our time, which is irreplaceable." – Jean-Louis Servan- Schreiber

"Fake it till you make it."- Tony Robbins

"The greater danger for most of us is not that our aim is too high and we miss it. But that it is too low... and we reach it." – Michelangelo 1475-1564

"Until you actually make a physical move and take action, all the dreaming and scheming in the world will get you nowhere near your vision."– Pat Croce

"The act of taking the first step is what separates the winners from the losers." - Brian Tracy

"Vision without action is a daydream – Action without vision is a nightmare." – Japanese proverb

"As I grow older, I pay less attention to what men say. I just watch what they do." – Andrew Carnegie

"The ultimate measure of a man is not where he stands in moment of comfort, but where he stands at times of challenge." - Martin Luther King Jr.

"Never have regrets, follow your heart." – Hillary Richards

"Put your future in good hands – your own." – Mark Victor Hanson

"How we spend our days is, of course, how we spend our lives." – Annie Dillard

"Listen to your dreams – those are the sounds no one else can hear." – Kobi Yamada

"You are the one who can stretch your own horizon." – *Edgar Maguin*

"Difficulties make you a jewel." – *Japanese proverb*

"It gets dark sometimes, but morning comes. Keep hope alive." – *Jesse Jackson*

"Either we have our dreams or we live our dreams." – *Zoë Koplowitz*

"Sticking to it is the genius ."– *Thomas Edison*

"Follow your heart even when others scoff. Don't be beaten down by naysayers." – *Howard Schultz*

"Dreams don't die until we let them." – *James Ojala*

"If you love life, do not squander time. That is the stuff life is made of!" – *Ben Franklin*

"Every moment of your life, including this one, is a fresh start." – *B J Marshall*

"Nobody who ever gave his best regretted it." – *George Halas*

"Change is not merely necessary to life; it is life." – *Alvin Toffler*

"Who are 'they' that hold so much power over our lives?" – *Orville Thompson*

"To find an open road, have an open mind." – *John Towne*

"You can do anything – but you can't do everything." – *David Allen*

"People can't answer a call that isn't made." – Robert Morgan

"Use your imagination not to scare yourself to death but to inspire yourself to life." – Adele Brookman

"If you want to do something, you find a way. If you don't want to do something, you find an excuse." – Dawn Bauer

"No one rises to low expectations." – Les Brown

"If you can't do it with feeling, don't." – Patsy Cline

"A single idea can transform a life, a business, a nation, a world." – Dan Zadra

"Don't wait to be discovered." – Gill Atkinson

"Learning is not compulsory, but neither is survival." – W Edwards Deming

"In a nation of millions and a world of billions, the individual is still the first and basic agent of change." – Lynden B Johnson

"Normal is not something to aspire to; it's something to get away from." – Jodie Foster

"If we always do what we always did, we will always get what we always got." – Jackie Mabley

"As long as I have to die my own death, I have decided to live my own life and not let others live it for me." – Hanoch McCarthy

"You're only given a little spark of madness. You mustn't lose it." – Robin Williams

"Think big thoughts, but relish small pleasures." – Jackson Brown Jr.

"Having fun is not diversion from a successful life; it is the pathway to it." – Martha Beck

"If you're not enjoying the journey, you probably won't enjoy the destination." – Joe Tye

"Enjoy yourself. These are the 'good old days' you're going to miss years ahead. We can never go back again, that much is certain." – B J Marshall

"Changing one small thing for the better is worth more than proving a thousand people wrong." – Anthony Pivec

"There will come a time when you believe everything is finished. That will be the beginning." – Louis L'Amour

"If you have knowledge, let others light their candles at it." – Margaret Fuller

"It is literally true that you can succeed best and quickest by helping others to success." – Napoleon Hill

"There is no such thing as a self-made person. You will reach your goals only with help of others." – George Shinn

"One day, in retrospect, the years of struggle will strike you as the most beautiful." – Sigmund Freud

"When you have confidence, you can have a lot of fun. And when you have fun, you can do amazing things." – Joe Namath

"Surround yourself with people who believe you can." – Dan Zadra

"Imagination is the preview of life's coming attractions." – Larry Eisenberg

"We are all born originals – why is it so many of us die copies." – Edward Young

"Time invested in improving ourselves cuts down on time wasted in disapproving of others." – Leona Green

"There is no such thing as expecting too much." – Susan Cheever

"People are always blaming their circumstances for what they are. I don't believe in circumstances. The people who get on in this world are the people who get up and look for the circumstances they want, and if they can't find them, they make them." - George Bernard Shaw

--

I like quotes so much, I started my own twitter account just to put some of the best quotes out on twitter that I can find. You can check it out here: www.twitter.com/MarkyQuotes

Sense and sensibility

A US businessman was at the pier of a small coastal Mexican fishing village when a small boat with just one fisherman docked. Inside the boat were several large yellow fin tuna. The American complimented the Mexican on the quality of his fish and asked how long it took to catch them.

The Mexican replied, "Only a little while, Señor." The American asked why he didn't stay out longer and catch more fish. The Mexican replied that he had enough to supply his family's immediate needs.

The American then asked, "But what do you do with the rest of your time?"

The fisherman said, "I play with my children, take siesta with my wife, Maria, stroll into the village each evening where I sup wine and play guitar with my amigos. I have a full and busy life, Señor."

The American smiled, "I have a Harvard MBA – that's a degree in business studies – I could help you. You should spend more time fishing and, with the proceeds, buy a bigger boat. With the proceeds from the bigger boat, you could buy several boats. Eventually you would have a fleet. Then instead of selling your catch to a middleman, you would sell directly to the processor, eventually opening up your own cannery. You would control the product, processing and distribution. You would, of course, need to leave this small coastal fishing village and move to Mexico City, then Los Angeles and eventually New York City where you would run your expanding enterprise."

The Mexican Fisherman asked, "But, Señor, how long would all this take?"

The American replied, "Fifteen to twenty years."

"But what then, Señor?"

The American laughed, "That's the best part. When the time is right, you sell your stock to the public and become rich. You would make millions."

"Millions, Señor? But then what?"

"Then you would retire, move to a small coastal fishing village, where you could sleep late, fish a little, play with your kids, take siesta with your wife, Maria, and stroll to the village in the evening where you could sup wine and play your guitar with your amigos."

With just the hint of a twinkle in his eyes, the fisherman said, "Señor, are these business degrees hard to get?"

You need to take exactly the right amount of action to get what you want. When you have what you want, you need to take exactly the right amount of action to keep your dream alive.

> ### Marky's Thought -
> *I used to be the US business type guy. Although I have a lot of ambitions, I am aware that if you are not careful, you can always be striving for things that end you back where you started. I think all my life experiences have taught me a great deal about sense and sensibility.*

Slow dance

Have you ever watched kids on a merry-go-round?
Or listened to the rain slapping on the ground?
Every followed a butterfly's erratic flight? Or gazed at the sun into the fading night?
You better slow down. Don't dance so fast.
Time is short. The music won't last.
Do you run through each day on the fly?
When you ask, "How are you?" Do you hear the reply?
When the day is done, do you lie in your bed,
With the next hundred chores running through your head?
You'd better slow down. Don't dance so fast.
Time is short. The music won't last.
Ever told your child, we'll do it tomorrow?
And in your haste, not see his sorrow?
Ever lost touch, let a good friendship die
'Cause you never had time to call and say, "Hi"?
You'd better slow down. Don't dance so fast.
Time is short. The music won't last.
When you run so fast to get somewhere, you miss half the fun of getting there.
When you worry and hurry through your day, it is like an unopened gift.... Thrown away....
Life is not a race. Do take it slower.
Hear the music. Before the song is over.

Marky's Thought -
I like this, I read it regularly. It reminds me of what life really means. After all, as Harry used to tell me, business is a game and money just keeps the score. I would add to that, life is a game too, and happiness just keeps the score.

> *Marky's Thought -*
> *Think about it; you can't change the past and tomorrow isn't here yet. All you can do is to live in the moment and live the best moment, second by second. I struggle with doing this sometimes myself, looking back at the past, (I only did it last night while writing some of this book) and sometimes I plan too much. It's a by-product of thinking too much. But I try hard now to live in the moment. After all, it's the only moment we have. The one right now.*

Life Tools

The more tools you can use in your life to help you achieve what you want to achieve, the better. I use tools every day to try and help me become more productive. I also try and read as much as I can. I believe reading, like travel, only has a positive effect for everyone. I mostly read non-fiction books and mainly personal development/business books. I thought I should share some here with you.

Books you should read

The Impact Code by Nigel Risner - This is one of my top five favourite books ever. Nigel has a great way of focusing you in on relevant things at the right time for you. I first read this book in 2007 and it helped me massively. I have read it another three times since. Get it in your life now.

The Power Of Focus by Jack Canfield - Great book for those of us that struggle to focus sometimes. I'm sure it will help you as much as it has helped me once you read it.

F**k It by John C Parkin - A very different book to many of my other suggestions. It gives a different perspective to life and how you may want to live it. In the top five books for me. Saying, "Fuck it," to things and to people is tremendously powerful.

The 4-Hour Work Week by Timothy Ferriss - You probably have heard about this book already. I read it when it first came out. It gives you a different way of thinking about how you can live the life you want without accumulating all the 'things' people feel they need to. It also sparks you into thinking about ways of making income streams without having to work in the normal way. If you haven't read it, you should.

How to Get Rich by Felix Dennis - Another top five book for me. I want to meet Felix one day. Felix Dennis is a British guy who has gone on to make hundreds of millions of pounds from publishing. This book is right to the point and tells it how it is. He has been there and done it and is, I must say, one of the few people I look up to. Read the book and it will make you laugh and, more importantly, think about what you really want and if you really want it enough. One of the best lessons from the book I learnt from the book is, "If it flies, floats or fornicates, always rent it."

S.U.M.O. (Shut Up, Move On) by Paul McGhee - This is a book everyone should read because, at some point in our lives, we are all guilty of wearing the victim T-shirt. Paul gets you on track and thinking right. Read it.

Chronic Marketer by Brad Gosse - Brad wrote this book in 2012 and put all his own opinions on life, business and marketing into it. If you want a refreshing take on what you should be doing and how you should be thinking, you should get this book. Now...

Courses you should get

Get the Edge by Tony Robbins - This is an audio programme and one of the best personal development courses I know of. I was lucky enough to attend Tony's *Unleash the Power Within* event in 2004 and it was life changing. His 'Get the Edge' audio course takes you on a personal journey that helps you to develop as a person. I quite often listen to it in my car. Get it in your life.

"Rich people have small TVs and big libraries, and poor people have small libraries and big TVs."
Zig Ziglar

More business and life tools

There are a bunch of tools, software and websites I use on a daily basis, too many to list here. You can see all of them and get direct access by going here:
www.marklyford.com/likes/bookupdates

"Social media spark a revelation that we, the people, have a voice, and through the democratisation of content and ideas we can once again unite around common passions, inspire movements, and ignite change."

Brian Solis, Engage: The Complete Guide for Brands and Businesses to Build, Cultivate, and Measure Success in the New Web

Twitter People

I love Twitter. I think it's about one of the best innovations on the Internet. This is a list of my favourite people I like to follow on Twitter for various reasons. See if you would like to follow any of them:

www.twitter.com/bradgosse
Brad is a great friend, early mentor and a business partner of mine. He has been around online since when I started, made a lot of money, and he and I share the same interest in online businesses and people. Brad's a vegan too (don't hold it against him); seriously. if you are a vegan or interested in veganism, you need to check him out too. Check outhis www.vectortunes.com site too.

www.twitter.com/nigelrisner
Nigel is my coach and mentor and the author of one of my favourite books of all time, *The Impact Code*. I introduced Nigel to Twitter; you should check him out and start following him.

www.twitter.com/1Password
I use 1Password to store all my passwords, web logins and secure information. It's a great app and runs on Mac and iPhone

www.twitter.com/37signals

37Signals run Basecamp. It's the best online collaboration software I know. We use it daily to collaborate all our businesses and projects.

www.twitter.com/_oddboy

Into tattoos? Matt 'Oddboy' Barrett-Jones is one of the best tattoo artists in the UK today; he did my Phoenix for me. If you want an appointment with him, be prepared to wait a while!

www.twitter.com/crofty666

Lee 'Crofty' Crofts is another other great tattoo artist. Lee is based in Leicester and did my Buddha for me. If you want a great tattoo, Crofty is your man.

www.twitter.com/Addictd2Success

Run by Joel Brown, this is one of the best Success and motivational Twitter feeds around. The website is amazing. Get it in your life.

www.twitter.com/billmaher

I love following Bill Maher on twitter. I watched some of his stand-up routines and started following him. Great views :)

www.twitter.com/BlurtAlerts

Run by the great Jayne. Blurt Alerts is the twitter feed of The Blurt Foundation; A great resource for raising awareness and dispelling the stigma of depression.

www.twitter.com/BradBurton

Brad runs one of the biggest business networking companies in the UK.

www.twitter.com/ChrisConeyInt

I first met Chris at a presentation skills day ran by @NigelRisner. Chris is a great guy and is all about people living a life of freedom.

www.twitter.com/DanielPriestley

I don't know Daniel personally but he runs the website www.keypersonofinfluence.com and is the author of the book *How to Become a Key Person of Influence* too.

www.twitter.com/DanielWagner

I have known Daniel for a few years now. He too has a compelling and interesting life story. He is an online marketing master too.

www.twitter.com/dot2uk

This guy does great design, in particular, he does some of the best avatars for people I have ever seen.

www.twitter.com/eBay_King

Lewis is the king of selling on eBay in the UK. He knows how to make money on eBay; well worth checking out.

www.twitter.com/Emergise

Emergise is run by Emma. She puts out some of the sweetest, motivational thoughts you will ever see. She and her Twitter feed will make you smile. :)

www.twitter.com/evernote

I use Evernote each and every day to organise my life, notes, thoughts and a whole lot more every day. Seriously, you need this in your life!

www.twitter.com/Wunderlist

Another program I use every day. I run my life using to-do lists and Wunderlist deals with them all for me. It runs on your iPhone, Android phone, Web, PC and Mac. If you use to-do lists, you need this.

www.twitter.com/FelixDennis

I have mentioned Felix Dennis throughout this book. His book *How to Get Rich* first got me interested in him. Well worth following on Twitter and worth checking out his website too!

www.twitter.com/garyvee

Gary Vaynerchuk loves to hustle. If you are an entrepreneur, you need to follow Gary.

www.twitter.com/irishmarketerv

Tony is a great guy, I first met him in London a few years ago. Well worth following.

www.twitter.com/JDEntrepreneur

Jamie Dunn is a young entrepreneur in the UK who is going places. Follow him.

www.twitter.com/joshewin

Joshy. My first ever employee. He has gone on to make a great success of his life. If you are into marketing, you should follow him.

www.twitter.com/kevinrose

The founder of Digg.com Kevin Rose is an online entrepreneur who loves tea. You should follow him if you like tech and new online technology.

www.twitter.com/KimDotcom

Founder of Mega Upload. In my opinion, Kim is a legend. Currently fighting a legal battle to avoid extradition to the USA, he is a freedom fighter in the online world. When you read about what Kim has had thrown at him for running a website that did no more than YouTube does each day, you will be amazed and should be interested to follow him. His new Mega company is going to be a massive success.

www.twitter.com/lifehacker

Lifehacker's website is somewhere I visit daily. Great information each day that will help your life.

www.twitter.com/nigelbotterill

Nigel is a UK-based entrepreneur who has created many multimillion pound companies. Well worth following for business insights.

www.twitter.com/NoteTakingNerd

My Note Taking Nerd is an amazing resource. Dexter runs it and the service he provides is a must for entrepreneurs looking to learn fast. He distils the biggest courses and seminars into simple to follow critical notes that allow you to learn quickly. A must in my opinion.

www.twitter.com/Paul_Clifford

Paul runs a great software company which produce some excellent products. You should check him out.

www.twitter.com/paulteague_uk

Paul is an ex-BBC guy, who now runs a very successful online software company, focusing on Facebook. Check him out.

www.twitter.com/petecraig

I have known my mate Pete for a few years now. Check him out.

www.twitter.com/richardbeldon

Richard is a local business marketing guy who runs a string of successful local magazine in Leicestershire. His 'let's go local' site is a great resource for businesses. Check him out.

www.twitter.com/RicheloKillian

Richello runs Imnica Mail. A great email auto responder service.

www.twitter.com/rickygervais

Love him or hate him, I love his twitter feed. I think he is one of the funniest men around. :)

www.twitter.com/rustyrockets

Russell Brand is well worth following on Twitter in my opinion. :)

www.twitter.com/simoncrabbuk

Simon is a mate of mine who I work with on different projects. Check him out.

www.twitter.com/SimonHodgkinson

One of my online friends and mentors. Simon has been online for over 10 years now and has made millions. Simon's marketing techniques and experience is second to none. He and his business partner Jeremy put out some of the best products I know.

www.twitter.com/SureFireWealth

Jeremy Gislason is Simon Hogkinson's business partner and runs some great marketing sites. A true legend within the online marketing community. His surefirewealth.com site is a treasure trove of information and products for anyone wanting to market their business online.

www.twitter.com/tferriss

Tim Ferriss is famous for his book *The 4-Hour Work Week*. Tim tweets some real interesting things about life and life design.

www.twitter.com/thefuckitlife

John C. Parkin is the author of *F**k It*. Following him on Twitter will give you some thought-provoking things to think about daily.

www.twitter.com/THEJamesWhale

One of my favourite talk show DJs ever. His weekly podcast is well worth getting.

www.twitter.com/thequote

If you love quotes like I do, you need to follow The Quote. One of the best quotes on your timeline you can get.

www.twitter.com/theRealKiyosaki

Author of *Rich Dad Poor Dad*. Follow Robert for tips and thoughts on investing and money.

www.twitter.com/TheRealSambora

The rock dog that is Richie Sambora. Lead guitarist with one of my favourite bands ever, Bon Jovi. I love Richie because he is real.

www.twitter.com/TheSumoGuy

Paul McGhee is the author of *S.U.M.O. (Shut up, Move on)*. Paul lives in the UK and helps people with his books and stage work. You need to read the book and get *S.U.M.O.* in your life.

www.twitter.com/tonyrobbins

Tony gave me my first taste of personal development in 2004 when I attended his UPW event in London. Tony has mastered what makes people tick, and how to motivate them. Check him out and get following him.

www.twitter.com/unmarketing

Scott Stratten is a marketing guy with a difference. He goes against the grain of what traditional marketing people say you should do. Follow him if you want marketing thoughts and ideas for your business.

www.twitter.com/ZedShah

Zed is a gent. One of the nicest guys I know. Plain and simple, you should check him out.

www.twitter.com/FrankTurner

Probably one of best UK musicians of our time in my opinion. I am addicted to his music and was lucky enough to meet him with my boys a few months ago. Nice guy who wears his heart on his sleeve through his music.

www.twitter.com/RealNewsTimes

I co-own Real News Now. It's a news site that tells it how it is.

www.twitter.com/BitBanx

My new Bitcoin business. Big things happening here. Follow us to keep track of our new Bitcoin enterprises.

www.twitter.com/GetSuccess

My own personal development site. Over the coming years, GetSuccess is going to grow as a brand and help as many people in the world as we can.

www.twitter.com/MarkyQuotes

My own personal quotes Twitter feed. The best quotes sent to your timelines daily. :)

Connect With Mark

Want to know or learn more? Then check out my website at www.marklyford.com or email me at mark@marklyford.com to find out what I am up to and how you can get involved. Also check online and at Amazon for more publications I am releasing over the coming months.

For more details of my businesses and websites visit: www.marklyford.com/thebusiness

****

Hit me up

It's easy to get in touch with me. The best way is to tweet me www.twitter.com/marklyford

Web: www.marklyford.com

Facebook: www.marklyford.com/facebook

Twitter: www.marklyford.com/twitter

YouTube: www.marklyford.com/youtube

****

Updates

Things change all the time in my life. I have put up an updates area so I can tell you about any things that change after I have written this book and it is in print. You can visit the updates site at www.marklyford.com/likes/bookupdates

****

Extras

I have included a reader's only extras area on my website. This includes some other digital resources for you to use and to help you along the way. All free for you as a reader of this book. To access the extra section, just go to www.marklyford.com/likes/bookextras

People To Thank

"Count your age by friends, not years. Count your life by smiles, not tears." John Lennon

I have many people to thank in my life. These are just a few. If I have missed you out, I apologise.

Mum and Dad - What can I say? You have both been my rock throughout my life. Without you both giving me the unconditional love and support throughout thick and thin, I don't know what I would have done. I can't say how much I appreciate you both and love you. Thank you for being the best mum and dad in the world. I really can't put into words how much I feel about you both, so I will shut up now. :)

Carl and Anne - Bro, it's been a ride, hey. Thanks for being a great brother and friend. Ups and downs all the way. Anne, thanks for being a great sister-in-law. Your support has meant the world to me over the last few years. Who'd have thought you would be the settled down one, Carl. ;)

James and Alexander - My boys, I can't say how blessed I am to have you both in my life. You have given me the strength to carry on during times I felt like giving up. Words can't describe what I feel about you both. I love you so much and thank you for both being how you are. Here is to the future for us all and I'm looking forward to going to the pub with you both and having a few beers in the time that is going to fly by in the coming years!

John and Dawn Jacques - What can I say? We met 11 years ago. You have been my best friends throughout. I can't say how grateful I am to you both for the friendship you have shown me. Through some of the hardest times in my life, you have both been there for me, no matter what. People like you don't come along very often and I am blessed to call you both my best friends. Even though you are the VOR and always right, Dawny ;) Johnny, crack open the expensive wine. ;)

Shaun and Denise - Auntie and Uncle, but best friends really. Thank you for all your support and help. It's been a ride, but it hasn't finished yet! ;)

Harry Dann - It's been way too long since you left us all. You were my first mentor and best mate. Fourteen years on, I still think of you all the time and still smile when I think of the times we had together. Here's to tycooning and corporate raiding, mate. I hope you're not laughing at me too much from where you are. ;)

Alan Ward - I have known you for over 20 years, mate. Since first trying to sell you pigeons for too much money, you and May have been good friends to me. I thank you for all your friendship and help over the years. You are both dear in my heart.

Stuart 'Stan' Stanger - During the 20 months we spent together, you become one of my best friends. That time we spent together meant a lot to me. We shared some pretty special times during the hardest period of our lives, which I won't ever forget. But I will beat you at chess one day. Keep staring at the stars, mate, I'll be looking at them too.

Nigel Risner - I first read your book in 2007, and it changed my life in a dramatic way during one of the worst times of my life. We have since become friends and you have helped and coached me as a friend and mentor since. I owe you a great deal.

Brad Gosse - We have known each other way too long now, Brad. We were there making it happen back in the 1990s and we have kept in touch since. A special thank you for helping me set back up again and get back on my feet after coming out of prison. You gave me the $20 to get started again. Thanks for all the listening, arse-kicking and help you gave me to get me back on track. I am very grateful, mate.

Simon Hodgkinson - You were one of the first people I met and looked up to when I started online again. Thanks for your help and support and the many hours on Skype helping and kicking me up the arse. Your friendship is much appreciated. Here's to the next mastermind meet-up!

My 'net' family - Soren Jordansen, Matt Garrett, Simon Hodgkinson, JP Schoeffel - 'The guys' - Thanks for taking me into your 'IM' drinking fold. I appreciate all your friendships and the great times we have spent together over the numerous weekends of 'masterminding'. P.S. Dave the dog says woof and, "hi". ;)

Peter Craig - You have been a good mate since we met in 2010. I appreciate our friendship and all the conversations we have had together, mate.

Michelle Craig - Thank you, Mikki, for trying to keep me organised. It's a hard job, I know. :)

Neil Stafford – Neil, thanks for making your own mind up about me and helping me with my online business since I started again. Your input and help has meant a lot to me.

Mark Anastasi – Mark, thank you for your support and help during some very difficult times in my life; your help has been much appreciated, mate.

George Fawcett - Thanks for giving me one of my first adult life experiences in Las Vegas, mate. You will always be a special friend to me.

Kate - My ex-wife. Although things didn't work out how either of us had hoped, I have to thank you for giving me two fantastic boys. We will be great parents together and I know the vision we both have of our boys will be a reality if and when they get married themselves. Thanks for giving me the most important people in my life and for the good times we shared during the good old days together. :)

There have been many other people who have influenced me in my life. Thanks to Anthony Robbins, Jack Canfield and Paul McGhee.

> *Marky's Thought -*
> *Friends and family are the most import things in your life. Appreciate them now and be thankful for all the great people you have in your life.*

Website Content

There are some good and bad things that happened in my life that are either too weird, sexual or just outright different that I have decided not to include in the main book, but people around me say I should include, as this book was always meant to be everything about my life. So I have decided to include those items as an optional extra on my website. It's up to you if you access them or not.

Warning though: All of the content is only suitable for over 18s and, in some cases, the content may offend some people. You have been warned! :)

To access this content, go here:
www.marklyford.com/likes/morestories

A thanks from Mark